IMPROVING TEACHER EDUCATION:

A

CONSCIOUS CHOICE

By

Johnnie Ruth Mills

Jo Ann Dauzat

Burnett Joiner

With
Contributions by

Jack Gant

Earline Simms

KENDALL/HUNT PUBLISHING COMPANY
2460 Kerper Boulevard   P.O. Box 539   Dubuque, Iowa 52004-0539

DEDICATION

Of and for our Colleagues and Students

at

Grambling State University

Copyright © 1989 by Kendall/Hunt Publishing Company

Library of Congress Catalog Card Number: 89–84462

ISBN 0–8403–5364–2

Printed in the United States of America
10 9 8 7 6 5 4 3 2 1

Acknowledgments

No one person changes a college, a university, or a system of teacher education. Thus no one person is responsible for what is written on these pages. This literary contribution represents the toil, patience, time, caring, sharing, and dreams of many individuals. Because these individuals are special, we, like other authors, wish to acknowledge them at this time.

The work of our colleagues in the College of Education and all across the campus of Grambling State University, the administration, President Joseph Johnson and Vice President Lamore Carter, provides the plot for this story. Without their quest for excellence, perseverance, and willingness to work and allow us to work and dream dreams, there would be nothing to tell. So first and foremost we wish to thank this gallant group for a job well done. Our hope is that we can continue together in beating the odds against excellence.

Several consultants gave of their talents and services to help the College survive, learn, and grow from its reform efforts. One consultant in particular, Jack Gant, was always there–taking our pulse, treating our organization ills, giving us therapy for change and development, and helping us learn to walk alone through our problems. His consultation, training, and professional insight guided, sustained and nourished us. We thank you, Jack.

Over the past eight years, many other consultants also contributed to the improvement of our teacher education program. They are: John Hansen, Walt LeBaron, Thelma Spencer, Arthur Whimbey, Gene George, Billy Slaughter, Reginald Corder, Charles Gifford, Fanchon Funk, Robert Crew, Michael Glisson, Linda Tarver, Richard Majetic, Larry Winecoff, Barbara Hatton, William Harris, Lois Hart, and David Imig.

A writing project of this magnitude is a difficult, complex process. It requires numerous support and clerical services from many talented people. We were fortunate to have such talent on our campus, to have access to people who not only wanted to cooperate, but also who took pride in helping. Our deepest gratitude for these support efforts is extended to: the late Claudia Terry, Walteree Barnes, Larry Lewis, Cynthia Rippie, Mary Schnuth, Selena McLaughlin, Fannie Belton, Wanda Dwight, Barbara Fowler, Hazel Earles, and Vickie Charles-Rogers, who spent many nights and weekends typing and retyping this manuscript.

FOREWORD

A Conscious Choice should be required reading for all who call themselves teacher educators. It is as applicable to private colleges and universities as to public, to institutions that historically enrolled only white students as it is to historically Black colleges and universities, and to research universities as to those that were initially intended to serve only a teacher education function. A Conscious Choice has significant lessons for each of us.

In 1978-79, eight of the 156 Grambling graduates who took the National Teacher Examination made passing scores; in 1985-86, approximately 35 of 40 Grambling graduates who took the NTE passed. Although the numbers were smaller in 1985-86 than they were in 1978-79, the number of students now enrolling in teacher education at Grambling State University is rapidly climbing back to where it was before the NTE was mandated for certification in Louisiana. A Conscious Choice relates what occurred in the intervening years to bring about the dramatic change in NTE scores. It tells of the trauma, the planning and doing, and the support given by a university administration that wanted its students to succeed, as well as by cooperative colleagues in liberal arts and education.

The final chapter of A Conscious Choice is titled "Program Outcomes and Lessons Learned," but almost every page in the entire volume contains an important message. A prefatory letter to teacher education colleagues, for instance, notes, "As a profession, we cannot afford to lose our Black teachers or our historically Black teacher-training institutions. But lose them we will if we continue doing nothing." And in Chapter 3 is the recognition that "Every new standard and set of actions for students meant reciprocal standards and action...for faculty members and administrators." Although most of us have experienced this, it was also good to be reminded that, when "Proposal developers, college administrators and the NTE Steering Committee thought that approval of the teacher education improvement proposal signaled readiness for implementation. They were wrong. Instead, approval elicited questions from faculty members who had remained dormant for months."

During the past 40 years, teacher education has come under repeated critical scrutiny. Some of our more forward-looking colleagues have been far ahead of the critics in instituting programs that warranted only approbation. More frequently, there has been substantial truth in the criticism. In those cases, we sometimes have responded by ignoring our critics, sometimes by aggressively defending our multiple virtues, and sometimes by hiding until the threat passed. In a few instances the criticism has been so serious that programs have found themselves in life-threatening circumstances. Grambling State University clearly was in this situation in 1980, but not everyone recognized it. Grambling's leaders in teacher education did, however, and with rare insight, they made a conscious choice to attack the problem, not the critics, and to develop a program of excellence in teacher education. Their choice led to hard work, to making everyone's role and responsibility public, to recognizing success, and to helping where failures occurred. The result was success.

We in teacher education must confront our own reluctance to change. We must seek to improve, to insist on ever higher standards from ourselves, our colleagues, and our students. Grambling has done that; they have established themselves as twentieth-century pioneers.

We must not misjudge the cost, however. What Grambling teacher educators have achieved took courage and hard work, and they still have a long way to go. Nevertheless, one cannot read this book without being instructed in what the rest of us should do and inspired to work at it.

Robert L. Egbert
George W. Holmes Professor of Education
University of Nebraska-Lincoln

PREFACE

This success story began about eight years ago when the College of Education at Grambling State University made a conscious choice to develop a program of excellence in teacher education. The desire was to take the present program and to make it better. The new program would reflect not only responsiveness to emergent societal forces such as teacher testing, but also responsiveness to changes in the knowledge base for teacher education caused by societal manipulations and research.

What was the catalyst for these new dreams? Foremost, the past scores of Grambling's preservice teachers on the National Teacher Examinations (NTE) suggested that students had acute knowledge and skill deficiencies in several academic areas. Moreover, consistent publicity of Grambling's high NTE failure rate in various newspapers nourished a negative public image of the institution's teacher training program. These reports, unfortunately, seemed to imply that Grambling and other similarly troubled institutions were unaffordable academic blights. Nationwide, talk of Black teacher incompetence and a possible need to dismantle historically Black institutions blistered the credibility of Black academicians, including those at Grambling. The message of the time seemed to have been, "We want Black teacher colleges out of business." Consequently, if Grambling's College of Education were to continue helping to meet society's educational needs, and if the college were to stay in business, observed student deficiencies would have to be remedied.

The monumental task of revamping Grambling's preservice teacher education program began in the fall of 1980. To increase the pass rate of preservice teachers on the NTE and to improve their general academic performance, six programmatic improvements were launched and implemented: student assessment, faculty development, curriculum revision, instructional development, program monitoring, and evaluation.

CONTENTS

4

OVERTURE FOR EXCELLENCE: TOWARD A PROGRAM
PLAN   **5 5**

Johnnie R. Mills

5

NO U-TURNS: COMPREHENSIVE CURRICULUM
REVISION   **6 6**

Jo Ann Dauzat

6

FACULTY DEVELOPMENT FOR EXCELLENCE   **7 8**

Jo Ann Dauzat

CONSULTANT'S NOTE #4: CARING FOR AN ORGANI-
ZATION IN TRANSITION   **8 5**

Jack Gant

7

MONITORING: STUDENT, FACULTY, AND CHANGE   **8 7**

Earline Simms

8

THE DEANSHIP: MAJOR PROBLEMS CONFRONTING

LEADERSHIP FOR ACADEMIC EXCELLENCE 100

Burnett Joiner

9

PROGRESS: PROGRAM OUTCOMES AND LESSONS LEARNED 109

Burnett Joiner

CONSULTANT'S NOTE #5: LOOKING FORWARD TO ORGANIZATIONAL INDEPENDENCE 124

Jack Gant

PRELIMINARY ASSUMPTIONS AND OBSERVATIONS

Several assumptions, confirmed in the research literature, undergirded Grambling's improvement efforts: (1) Test scores had implications for what was learned as well as for what was taught (Burke and Stoltenberg, 1979; Ebel, 1975; Gross, 1979; Pipho, 1979; and Report on Education Research, May 28, 1980). (2) It was one thing to be competent, but another to demonstrate competence on a test. (3) Just as students should be trained in and sensitized to test taking, so should curricula be sensitive to their needs for test-taking skills (Gross, 1979; Gubser, 1979; Pottinger, 1979). This sensitivity, the experts claimed should encompass subject matter retention **and** practical experiences in reasoning, problem solving, application of content, and test taking. Acknowledging that some students fail tests for reasons other than lack of knowledge or lack of competence also was suggested. For many students, it was concluded, failure simply results from the absence of academic emphasis on performance that demonstrates competence on pencil-paper tests.

Grambling believed that NTE scores would increase as chasms (conceptual and methodological) in the training curriculum for preservice teachers were closed. Early prognosis for a cure maintained that, at minimum, adjustment to existing course designs might be needed. In all probability, wholesale curriculum revision would be mandatory.

What should be the nature of curriculum revision? Klemp (1977) pinpointed three broad dimensions of performance (cognitive processing, interpersonal skills, and motivation) that seemed highly related to competence, but which rarely were a part of any formal curriculum or evaluative procedures in postsecondary education. He also saw the type of cognitive skills applied during knowledge acquisition and problem solving, rather than the actual acquisition or use of knowledge, as better indicators of outstanding performers.

Essentially, information processing skills seemed less important to successful performance than conceptual skills which helped to harmonize the disorganized information schemes which typify everyday environments. If, suggested Klemp, personal attributes such as empathy, maturity, well-developed cognitive processes, ability to think clearly under stress, moral reasoning abilities, interpersonal effectiveness, and motivation are considered important aspects of competence, then these areas must be addressed in training curriculum and evaluative processes. This reasoning seemed applicable to Grambling's problem. If its preservice teachers were to demonstrate increased competence in taking teacher tests, classroom instruction, communicating, conceptualizing and reasoning to solve problems, then its curriculum would have to reflect such concerns as well.

The eight years following Grambling's 1980 decision to pursue excellence in teacher training have witnessed the development of many innovative ideas, practices and products; none of which came easily. They emerged from bare-bones budgets and overworked dreamers who believed it possible to turn the College around. They emerged from the struggles of faculty, students and administrators who, at the same time, had to live with the trauma of change. Forces such as personnel changes, faculty-perceived autonomy and course ownership, and resistance to changing encrusted traditional structures and behaviors frequently operated to undermine improvement efforts. Ultimately, these forces were transformed into constructive energy that netted the College many benefits.

OVERVIEW OF PROGRAM OUTCOMES AND BENEFITS

Beyond a renewed curriculum, Grambling now enjoys an increasing enrollment, an improved pass rate on the NTE, improved faculty morale, and a proven model for realizing excellence in teacher education. The conscious choice of excellence has rewarded Grambling in other ways, too. For example, in 1985 the College of Education received the American Association of State Colleges and Universities Showcase of Excellence Award in Teacher Education; the American Association of Colleges for Teacher Education featured Grambling at its 1985 Annual Meeting as a "leader meeting the challenge of change;" the Fund for the Improvement of Postsecondary Education funded a project for Grambling to validate and document its change program; the program won the 1987 Southeastern Regional Association of Teacher Educators award for innovation in teacher education; and currently, public opinion of Grambling is more positive.

An article on Grambling in the March 1985 issue of Higher Education Daily raised the question, "What accounts for this historically Black college's success story?" Numerous institutions have contacted the college asking the same question, seeking technical assistance, or requesting program description. This publication responds to these queries from the profession.

CHAPTER 1

EXCELLENCE: IN SEARCH OF MEANING

Grambling State University: A Success Story

> *Five years ago, only 10 percent of Grambling State University's teacher education graduates passed the National Teachers Exam (NTE). Today, some 80 percent of the graduates pass the test on their first attempt.*

> *Enrollment in the Louisiana school's teacher training program also has rebounded. In 1973 the school boasted an enrollment of 1,100 students, but five years ago it dropped under 300. Today, it is on the upswing with 800 full-time students.*

> *What accounts for this historically Black college's success story?*

> *Greg MaCaffery*
> *Higher Education Daily*
> *March 5, 1985*

THE CONTEXT OF CHANGE

Grambling State University (GSU) is a small, rural, historically Black institution in North Central Louisiana. It is one of two such public institutions in the state. Open admission policies and Grambling's history of taking students where they are and transforming them into productive citizens have attracted varied levels of students from across the nation. Primarily, though, the typical freshman is a Black student victimized by previous economic, educational, and social disadvantages. Of the institution's almost 6,000 students, approximately 90 percent receive some form of financial aid.

Until recently Grambling was most recognized nationally and internationally for its football accomplishments and the band's high-stepping performances. During the early eighties, the university also became known for its court struggles with state and federal governments to advance equity for Blacks in higher education.

Though less renown, Grambling's teacher education program also has a proud and illustrious history. The university began as a teacher training college.

1

Through the years it has distinguished itself in the state as a leader in developing innovative teacher training models (Jeanes teachers, supervision of first-year teachers, the master teacher). Growth and progress prompted the demise of Grambling as solely a teacher training institution, while transforming it into a comprehensive degree-granting university. As a result, the College of Education– with three academic departments, numerous undergraduate and graduate degree programs, and a K-12 laboratory school program–became one of several such organizational units.

Ninety-eight percent of the faculty in the College of Education have terminal degrees representing some of the most prominent institutions of America. Recognizing the importance of professional involvement, these faculty members hold offices and membership in a multiplicity of state, regional, and national organizations. While some members can claim articles in refereed journals, others serve proudly as referees and editors for a variety of professional publications.

As it is at many other historically Black colleges, faculty members in the College of Education at Grambling have worked through the years to perfect teaching strategies. They have considered themselves experts in curriculum development and instruction. They would be the first to admit, however, that in the past, while they were critics of poor research, they also were only consumers of good research. Teaching was their first priority.

The confrontation with troubled times, reforms, and change occurring in 1980 was nothing new to the education faculty. Historically, it had survived many similar adversities; but public indictment because of poor student performance on standardized competency tests was met with great trepidation. Failure rates of 80 to 90 percent for Grambling's graduates on the National Teacher Examinations (NTE) for initial teacher certification seemed totally to disarm faculty members. This was an affront to their credibility. Capsules of student data (Tables 1, 2, and 3) which show a comparative picture of Louisiana's institutional scores on the NTE over a three-year period, explain the faculty's discomfort.

TABLE 1

NATIONAL TEACHER EXAMINATION STATISTICS FOR LOUISIANA
1978-79

Louisiana Institutions	Number of Students taking NTE	Number of Students Passing	Number of Students Failing
Grambling	156	8	148
LSU-BR	311	254	57
LSU-Shreveport	34	33	1
Louisiana Tech	172	124	48
McNeese	181	104	77
Nicholls	176	99	77
Northwestern	138	85	53
Southeastern	211	123	88
Southern	134	2	132
Southern-NO	30	4	26
USL	230	161	69
UNO	192	162	30
Bap. Christian	8	5	3
Centenary	28	24	4
Dillard	*	*	*
La. College	64	49	15
Loyola	27	21	6
Holy Cross	62	41	21
St. Mary's Dom.	24	20	4
Tulane	23	23	0
Xavier	37	7	30
TOTAL	**2,409**	**11,451**	**958**
		60%	40%

TABLE 2

NATIONAL TEACHER EXAMINATION STATISTICS FOR LOUISIANA
1979-80

Louisiana Institutions	Number of Students taking NTE	Number of Students Passing	Number of Students Failing
Grambling	148	9	139
LSU-BR	244	203	41
LSU-Shreveport	45	40	5
Louisiana Tech	105	76	29
McNeese	122	89	33
Nicholls	129	86	43
Northwestern	166	113	53
Southeastern	105	71	34
Southern	185	102	83
Southern-NO	58	7	51
USL	165	110	55
UNO	173	157	16
Bap. Christian	8	5	3
Centenary	16	12	4
Dillard	*	*	*
La. College	42	34	8
Loyola	32	26	6
Holy Cross	45	37	8
St. Mary's Dom.	33	22	11
Tulane	49	49	0
Xavier	15	7	8
TOTAL	**1,925**	**1,258**	**667**
		65%	*35%*

TABLE 3

NATIONAL TEACHER EXAMINATION STATISTICS FOR LOUISIANA
1980-81

Louisiana Institutions	Number of Students taking NTE	Number of Students Passing	Number of Students Failing
Grambling	69	18	51
LSU-BR	224	189	35
LSU-Shreveport	29	27	2
Louisiana Tech	95	80	15
McNeese	102	72	30
Nicholls	120	87	33
Northwestern	144	95	49
Southeastern	58	42	16
Southern	143	93	50
Southern-NO	69	14	55
USL	161	118	43
UNO	139	127	12
Bap. Christian	5	2	3
Centenary	16	11	5
Dillard	10	7	3
La. College	48	39	9
Loyola	24	19	5
Holy Cross	24	22	2
St. Mary's Dom.	17	13	4
Tulane	23	22	1
Xavier	*	*	*
TOTAL	**1,555**	**1,105** 71%	**450** 29%

Usually the context of change in any organization transcends demographic and historical information. It extends to the perceptions, attitudes, and feelings of the people involved. Hence, a sample of these qualitative indicators seems appropriate here.

Though dampened in spirit by attacks on the college's credibility, some faculty members seemed to have doubted the quality of the teacher training program for a long time. Apparently not surprised at Grambling's plight was the professor who shared these feelings: "We have made many significant contributions to the profession, but also we have been sinking for years without a sense of direction."

When asked recently to reflect upon what the faculty's 1980 commitment to excellence actually meant, another professor stated:

> *It meant that we challenge ourselves. There was nothing out there to show us the way. Not one other historically Black college was doing better, or could serve as a model for us. There was not positive challenge from the State Department or the Board of Regents. In fact, in 1980 we were in a surplus situation with no one really wanting us to survive. I think the faculty knew this. And because they are survivors, their commitment was a commitment to survival, their own and the College's. The new dean motivated us to make such a commitment.*

It is a mistake to conclude that when the decision for excellence was made, and throughout subsequent struggles toward goal achievement for that matter, the situation would be conflict-free and one of faculty accord. Conversely, the decision for excellence was also a decision for change. This revelation split the faculty into several identifiable groups. One group strongly opposed the consideration of alternative approaches to teacher training. These resisters were fanatically protective of the traditional ways of operating and seemed to have felt that if everyone just put more emphasis on existing operations, everything would be okay. Led by one or two senior administrators and faculty members, this group met all suggestions for change with one of these favorite cliches: "Grambling has been doing that for years," or "This is nothing new to Grambling." Under the same leadership, resisters frequently embarked upon elaborate public campaigns to (a) sabotage new projects, (b) discredit the new dean and new faculty members, (c) plant seeds of distrust among other faculty members and between the College of Education and other academic units, and (d) embarrass and harass supporters of improvement efforts–all under the pretense of "loving Grambling."

6

Like most institutions, Grambling also had its share of those "retirees on the job." Faculty members in this second group were chary about supporting change efforts because it meant extra work–or work, period. While the retirees did little to sabotage improvement efforts, they spent themselves attempting to discern how to avoid participating or how to get others to do their assigned tasks for them.

Then there were the critics. Observations by this group seemed neither well-intended nor constructive. Rather, they appeared to be cries of anguish and disgust over the college's failure to respond to their personal demands and needs. Through arrogant, negative opinions, this group demonstrated a penchant for high-quality hindsight and a low tolerance for work. When asked for help or ideas at the start of the improvement effort, group members usually withheld assistance. Interestingly, the attitudes and public displays of the critics fed the fires set by resisters.

Finally, there was a group of supporters–faculty members who willingly and unselfishly worked despite the overwhelming nature of the task, the opposition from peers, and the work overload spawned by nonworking peers. Though originally small, the membership of this group gradually grew with converts from the preceding three groups and the addition of new faculty members.

To be sure, much conflict evolved because of the diverse nature and self-proclaimed missions of the groups just described. This conflict, in turn, led to the jockeying of group membership by faculty members. Consequential to these maneuvers was the constant formation of new secondary groups and restructured memberships for the four major groups. But not all conflict was bad for the improvement program, regardless of the motivation behind it. In reflection, professional conflict and some stressful situations strengthened the program and the people involved. Determination, exchange of ideas, and clarity of purpose were outcomes of such interactions. Interpersonal or personality conflicts, of which there were many, served only to make the college's work more difficult and to impede the personal growth of individuals.

In sum, destructively low morale, disbelief of the notion that the college (with its new dean) could turn things completely around, and lack of knowledge about how to get started on problem solutions permeated college halls and faculty offices for many months. These obstacles, along with ongoing internal organizational conflict (or infighting), initially blocked getting ideas off paper and into action in a timely manner. Only a small cadre of dedicated professionals who believed that hard work would pay off and saw some hope for the college were able to produce visible signs of progress early on. The dean seemed to understand the faculty's infantile stages of immobilizing stage fright, but he also knew that success would demand more than the work of a few. All minds and hands would be needed. A critical task for him, throughout the improvement program was crisis management–effectively resolving conflict while simultaneously influencing people to work toward priortized objectives and emergent problems.

How did the faculty arrive at its commitment to excellence? The answer to this question is unfolded in an account of the college's first significant goal setting event.

THE CHOICE: EITHER YELL AND SCREAM OR FACE REALITY

*"We have a problem. Either we solve that
problem or we will be forced to get out of
the business of training teachers."*

With these words to his faculty, the new dean of education at Grambling State University opened the first meeting of the 1980-81 academic year. The dean's message was not an indictment of the college's previous contributions to teacher education, but a conclusion drawn from several persuasive sources, including conversations with university and government officials around the state and country on future-funding priorities. It was the unavoidable implication drawn from analyzing trend data on student performance. The dean's message reflected his decisions between two choices: Either yell and scream about the injustices of teacher testing, or face reality. He chose recognizing reality–poor student performance and the negative consequences of such performance on tests; this was reality.

Thus, administrative mandates, the threat of losing state funds, and the 80 to 90 percent failure rate of its graduates on the NTE were the external motivators that spurred Grambling seriously to seek alternatives for improving student performance. At this first meeting, the intrinsic motivation of some faculty members surfaced and spread to their peers. By the end of the meeting, the faculty had made a conscious choice to meet the challenge of excellence in teacher education. But what did such a choice mean?

To the faculty, poor student performance seemed symptomatic of a much bigger problem, so achieving excellence meant more than just helping students to pass a test. Primary to its definition was taking a proactive, rather than the usual reactive, program development posture; acquiring high quality resources, students, and faculty; implementing an innovative curriculum that was sensitive to the remedial and enrichment needs of students; and building a learning climate capable of stretching the academic creativity of students and faculty. The position taken by the faculty will become clearer in subsequent passages.

The dean's first formal meeting of 1980 offered many faculty members a first opportunity to hear his ideas and to assess his acceptability as a leader. It is uncertain, however, that faculty completed their assessments of the dean on this occasion. The dean's message was brief. He introduced the problem of student performance and the three consultants he had brought in to diagnose the college's ills, then turned the faculty over to the consultants.

As faculty members drank coffee, ate donuts, and interacted with colleagues during the meeting, it became apparent that they saw students' test performance as only part of the problem. The concerns they aired to the consultants ranged from dysfunctional policies to poor instruction; from a lack of teaching supplies to poor student morale; from being ignored by the state department and higher education boards to grade inflation; from a lack of academic support services for students to the failure of other academic units to prepare students adequately; from no curriculum in some training areas to antiquated and redundant curriculum in other areas.

Despite the identification of instruction as a causal factor for students' poor performance, the faculty generally felt that students were, in part, responsible for their own deficiencies. Some faculty members cited, in example, that the reason students failed the NTE or failed to perform well in academic subjects was because they were unmotivated, because they had poor study habits, or because they entered the teacher education program with abundant remediation needs. In the same vein, other faculty members shared that students seldom completed reading assignments and failed to follow through on suggestions for getting help in the various remediation centers on campus. Forcing students to study or to utilize available resources was viewed as an impossibility, given the student monitoring process in use at that time.

Although some faculty members reported attempts to remediate when possible, they felt student weaknesses were too intense and burdensome for them to correct, considering the content they were charged with covering. To support this observation one faculty member stated:

> *In fact, it appears that if the trend toward increased remediation continues, the primary mission of Teacher Education will be drastically altered: from providing professional skills training to providing training in the basic skills. This is an alteration we can ill afford. However, it is true that the deficiencies students bring to us and our inability to be all things to all students probably explain the poor performance of these students on the NTE.*

When consultants eventually asked: Where is the college? Where do you want the college to go? What will it take to get there? And how can you as faculty members hold each other accountable? Faculty members answered. They seemed to have known intuitively that they had rested too long. In a momentous decision

9

they challenged themselves, and were bound by group consensus, to take control of the situation and the college's destiny. The choice of excellence was the challenge to cure those ills everyone knew existed, the ones they had just discussed. Consequently, what began as just another gripe session on this first day of the semester ended as a comprehensive needs assessment and long-term verbal commitment by faculty that was to span more than half a decade.

Immediately following this first meeting, several activities were initiated to keep the new goal alive in the minds of faculty members until more concrete action could be taken. Disseminating a report that summarized findings from the meeting was the first move the dean made. Subsequent initiatives included: research projects, a comprehensive NTE improvement proposal, the organizing of a College of Education Council and an NTE Steering Committee, development of departmental objectives and action plans, and the redesign of the existing testwiseness strategy. These planning tools and products, the first of many to come, brought about outcomes that eventually led to the success story acknowledged in the opening quote of this chapter. Moreover, through additional faculty retreats, think tanks, staff development, shared decision making and administrative assignments, most of those on the periphery of change were convinced to become involved.

THE FIRST SIGNS OF SUCCESS

The college saw the first significant change in student performance on the NTE during the summer of 1982. Sixty percent of the students who took the test met state certification standards. Isolation of any one stratagem used by the college to cause this modicum of success is impossible. Many improvement projects were going on simultaneously: curriculum revision, diagnostic-prescriptive instruction, development of testwiseness materials, faculty development on test construction, competition for external funds, development of an education resource center, field testing of new ideas, simulated NTE tests, and of course,–MEETINGS!

Upon the return of faculty members from summer vacation, the college celebrated its accomplishment at another one-day faculty retreat, this time off campus. Major differences between this activity and the one in 1980 were threefold. First, a primary purpose of the 1983 activity was to reinforce and to reward effective action, whereas the earlier agenda centered upon assessing ineffective action. Second, participating faculty members approached the 1983 activity with an increased sense of direction for achieving excellence. And third, more faculty members left the 1983 activity feeling a sense of achievement, believing that the college could be saved, and wanting to commit to action.

Near the close of the 1983 retreat, "Where are we?" was the question used to facilitate a progress check. The faculty's answers functioned as intrinsic motivation for them to continue their efforts. Later the faculty was admonished by the attending consultant to avoid being lulled into a false sense of security.

College administrators perceived the successful outcome of the retreat as another indicator of the college moving one step closer to excellence. Nonetheless, the administrators also were aware that they could not afford to rest on the retreat's perceived positive outcomes. Attention turned almost immediately to projects promising multiple benefits. First, a public image campaign was launched. As part of the campaign two major conferences were hosted by the college, one on testwiseness, the other on supervision. Curriculum revision and all other program development continued as planned, as replanned, and as replanned again–always toward refinement and improvement.

BEFORE AND AFTER SNAPSHOTS

The College of Education at Grambling has consistently enjoyed an increase in the scores of graduates on the NTE since 1982. The same holds true for the college's enrollment. These were concrete observable gains. To illustrate this fact are sample before and after newspaper excerpts.

Graduates do poorly on exam

BATON ROUGE (AP) — Education graduates from Grambling and Southern continue to do poorly on the examinations which must be passed if they are to teach in Louisiana public schools, records showed.

None of the 18 December education graduates from Grambling passed the National Teacher Examination while only three of 11 Southern graduates made the approved score for certification, the Department of Education records showed.

A report, compiled by the department, shows a continuing trend among the education graduates from those schools toward choosing not to take the examination.

Last December 107 students were eligible for the test at the two schools but only 29 took it.

Here is a rundown on results last December from other universities:

At Louisiana State University in Baton Rouge, 81 made passing scores out of the 93 students taking the examination; at LSU-Shreveport, all 13 students passed; at Louisiana Tech, 17 of 22 passed; McNeese State, 28 of 40.

Nicholls State, 31 of 48 passed; Northeast Louisiana University, 37 of 48; Northwestern State University, 20 of 25; Southeastern, 49 of 84; Southern University at New Orleans, 2 of 7; University of Southwestern Louisiana, 45 of 62; University of New Orleans, 40 of 49.

Voter registration

Voter registration in Louisiana has topped two million for the first time, state officials said Thursday.

—*Page 3*

High number of summer graduates pass NTE

BATON ROUGE — About two-thirds of the summer education graduates at three northeastern Louisiana universities who took the National Teachers Examination passed, according to figures released Thursday by the state Department of Education.

Statewide, nearly two-thirds of the summer education graduates eligible to take the NTE passed.

Figures from the three northeastern Louisiana schools were:

Grambling, 19 education graduates, 19 taking the test, 3 passing for 15 percent; Louisiana Tech, 30, 22, 16 for 72 percent; and Northeast Louisiana University 56, 56, 42 for 75 percent.

"This is the highest percentage of success we've had," said Dr. Bernard Shadoin, dean of NLU's College of Education. "I don't know if it's because we're doing anything different."

Shadoin said he has always favored "some kind of exit examinations" for education graduates, but was unsure the NTE, which the state began requiring in 1978, was the best alternative.

"I feel the selection was made quite hurriedly," he said. "I'm not convinced this (the NTE) is the best test."

Superintendent of Education J. Kelly Nix said the 290 new teachers helped ease a possible teacher shortage in several areas of the state. Education graduates can't teach in Louisiana without passing the test.

In a statement, the department said 74 percent of the graduates who took the test — 230 of 307 — passed. Some 43 education majors who were eligible didn't take the test, and figuring them in the passing per-

centage was 66 percent. Education graduates can't teach in the state without passing the NTE.

However, the figures are incomplete because there were no reports from four predominantly black schools — Southern-New Orleans, Dillard, Xavier and Southern-Baton Rouge. In the past, only a few education graduates of the four schools passed the test.

It was the second straight reporting period in which Southern-New Orleans, Xavier and Dillard failed to reveal how their education graduates did on the NTE or how many took it. In the spring, only two of 104 Southern-Baton Rouge graduates took the test — and both failed to pass.

Nix said the 74 percent passing ratio for those taking the test was up 10 percent from the figures for summer graduates a year ago.

He said there is still an insufficient number of certified teachers in certain academic areas for some local school systems, particularly in special education. Vacancies in special education and science have always been difficult to fill, he added.

"Add the fact that we had 2,292 teachers retire last year compared to the usual average of 900 per year, and you can see why some school systems may have difficulty filling certain positions," he said.

He said the 74 percent of those taking the test this year have passed, compared to 67 percent in 1979. In 1978, the first year the NTE was administered, 53 percent of the graduates scored high enough to be certified.

Nix said one of the reasons many of the teacher training programs have had an

increased number of students certified is that colleges and universities have taken steps to upgrade their programs.

Six programs had all of their summer graduates pass the NTE, including Tulane and LSU-Shreveport. It marked the second straight reporting period that all Tulane graduates taking the test passed.

Grambling had the lowest pass ratio of any of the reporting schools. Only three of the 19 education graduates — 15 percent — made the required score on the NTE. The ratio, however, was up from the 6 percent reported for spring graduates of Grambling.

As in the past, more private university graduates passed than those from state schools. Eighty-one percent of the private school education graduates passed, compared to 73 percent in the public system.

Cynthia Tucker

Grambling's College of Education points the way

The bad news comes as no surprise. Any attentive observer could have predicted that black teachers would not do well on the Georgia Teachers Certification Test.

Standardized tests have long been the bane of black folks. The controversy does not stop with teachers and students. You will recall that black officers of the Atlanta Police Bureau fared poorly with a recent standardized test required for promotion.

Sixty-two percent of the veteran black teachers who took the GTCT in Georgia in September failed it. The results in this state track closely the results in others. In Arkansas, the high failure rates were in counties with largely black populations.

The failure of Georgia's veteran black teachers also bears comparison with the failure rates of black students trying to enter the teaching profession. Around the country, 65 percent of blacks trying to get certified as teachers fail the test the first time. Only 13 percent of whites fail the first time. Teachers-in-training at predominantly black Fort Valley State and Albany State have had particular difficulty trying to pass the teacher certification exam.

Some believe standardized tests like the GTCT are racially biased; Hispanics also have difficulty passing such tests. But might there be another explanation? Many experts think the failing may lie in the inadequate education of many minority students and professionals. The recent history of the teacher education program at predominantly black Grambling State University in Grambling, La., is illuminating.

In 1977, the Louisiana legislature decreed that all college graduates trying to become schoolteachers must pass the National Teachers Exam. That first year, *95 percent of Grambling's students in the College of Education failed the test.*

What did Grambling do then? "We accepted the fact that we had to improve our overall performance," said Dr. Burnett Joiner, dean of the College of Education, "or we'd lose the program. Students would not want to come into a program that couldn't get them certified."

Yes, there were initial attempts to resist the testing requirement. Grambling joined other black schools that "fought or questioned" the test, Joiner said.

But later, "we decided we would not spend our energies fighting the test. The test was reality. While we will continue to question the test, to conduct research to determine whether the test

is the appropriate instrument to decide whether a person will be a good teacher, the reality that we are faced with is that our students must pass the test. It's a matter of priorities."

Grambling revamped the curriculum in its school of education, as well as strengthening the curricula in the schools of Liberals Arts and Science and Technology. The school of education hired new faculty members. It also began requiring education students to pass two portions of the NTE before they were permitted to take junior and senior level courses. Now, *80 percent of Grambling's education graduates pass the NTE,* giving Grambling one of the highest success rates in the state.

Joiner says three things are critical: The university's faculty and administration must commit to excellence and provide the resources, i.e. money, necessary to attain it; students have to know that the faculty and administration have high expectations of them; there has to be continuous assessment of students before they enter the education program and after they've been admitted.

He added, "When students are not able to negotiate the requirements, you must give them a chance. If they don't show the energy or ability to negotiate the requirements, you must put them out of the program."

Isn't Grambling's approach worth trying?

QUALITATIVE INDICATORS

Evidence of Grambling's success exists in more than just concrete form. Qualitative or abstract indicators, less talked about than the concrete but equally valuable, also exist. Grambling's public image improved as did faculty morale. The following describes how Grambling knew that such changes occurred.

Before 1983, Grambling's name appeared frequently but unfavorably in newspaper headlines. Most of these articles described test scores that were statistically true, but the subtle messages were false and destructive: "This is to be expected of Black colleges." "If you attend this college or others like it, you will be unable to qualify for a job upon graduating." "The incompetent Black teachers such colleges produce cause our public schools to do poorly with educating our children." "To close these colleges is to save tax dollars." In other words, it seemed that Grambling's College of Education was perceived as just another historically Black "degree mill" whose graduates were having problems with standardized tests–something to be expected.

As test scores began to creep up in 1983, public opinion (as measured by the media, the profession, members of the college's network, and personal contacts) was mixed. People simultaneously seemed baffled, disbelieving, relieved, and proud. Newspaper headlines began to change, but with caution and in an obvious pattern. To start, Grambling's name appeared less in the titles of articles and with little mention of improvement in the narratives that followed; later scores from Grambling were just one set among the others. The next series of articles mentioned the improved scores but raised questions about fewer students electing to take the test. The last two series of articles (a) highlighted Grambling's revamped program with little attention to Grambling having the second highest scores in the state, and (b) again put Grambling's name in the headlines, this time with a more positive ring. Concurrent with the changing newspaper headlines in Louisiana, things began to happen elsewhere. Newspapers across the southeastern United States acknowledged Grambling's achievement, and a major magazine negotiated to do a special report on the College of Education.

Proven success, however, does not always quickly snuff out the fires of disbelievers. Many embers of doubt remained despite Grambling's turn around. That many students were officially called upon by ETS to defend their NTE scores and that many outsiders continued to point up the college's weaknesses are but two examples. Nonetheless, consistent increases in students' test performances could not be ignored. So Grambling, understanding that success breeds suspicion, took these reprehensible acts as evidences of success too.

In addition to observed increases in appreciative public opinion and student enrollment, the Grambling network fostered some other qualitative and serendipitous image gains for the college. This network, seeded and cultivated by college administrators to prevent the college from becoming a closed system, comprises other institutions, professional groups, political bodies, and research organizations. From members of the network have come requests for technical assistance, collaborative projects, workshops, conference presentations, site visits, and interviews. Further, major research institutions within the network have included the college as a partner in proposed research undertakings.

The qualitative benefits of Grambling's improvement program initially were, and still are, observable in the feelings, perceptions, and attitudes of faculty members and students. As preservice teachers noticed that more of their peers were passing the NTE, they began to dress and act differently. The change in dress was particularly noticeable in the college's professional teaching seminar. Sports and casual clothes were shed for professional attire. Taking one or no books to class changed to taking attaches´ and zippered cases stuffed with several books and relevant news articles. Even more fundamental to solving the problem, students who once ran away from remedial assistance began to seek out such support services. Attendance at special study or information sessions also increased.

Equally as noteworthy, students who had graduated but still had the NTE to master and students from other institutions came to the college's NTE study sessions and to the Education Resource Center for practice on simulated NTE tests. Of Grambling's graduates, most already held temporary teaching positions. A survey of Louisiana principals revealed that Grambling's graduates were well respected for their classroom performance, regardless of their test scores.

Behavioral changes also transcended the College of Education's faculty. Besides revising general education curriculum toward sensitivity to the testing needs of students, more faculty members in the College of Liberal Arts and the College of Science and Technology began to attend education workshops. Though invited in the past, few had ever attended. It was also observed that these visiting faculty members invested more time in reviewing sample NTE tests and in redesigning their own tests to reflect the content and structure of the NTE.

OWNERSHIP IN SUCCESS DOES NOT NEED TO BE SOLD

It took less time for people to buy into the College of Education's success than it did for them to buy into its problems or its plans for solution. This reaction was to be expected. The central administration recognized the college's success during assemblies and university faculty meetings, and the responses were overwhelming. The earth-shattering applause was momentary, but residual benefits to the college were long-term.

In the months to follow, the college conducted many activities that ultimately infringed upon the time of all academic units across the campus. Surprisingly, the college met little or no opposition and, in fact, some support. In prior years, these units would have balked; now their faculty members offered more time, talent, and resources to improvement efforts. The university's administration also institutionalized across the campus new support activities that would have direct implications for improving the academic abilities of all students, regardless of their majors. These activities included general education seminars, departmental tests, comprehensive senior examinations, and university-sponsored monitoring of student performance through systematic evaluation and research.

TOWARD A BETTER UNDERSTANDING

This introductory chapter to the Grambling success story provides an overview of how the College of Education moved from visions of excellence to realization of its goal. But this slight treatment of change falls short of the substantial information needed to understand fully the Grambling model. It leaves intact the question: What did the College really do? The answer requires an in-depth exploration of program components and procedures. It requires looking at how objectives were operationalized, how emerging problems were solved, how program improvement activities were managed, and how training materials were used.

The following narrative describes what Grambling did to operationalize its objectives for each major component. It also shares insights intended to be helpful to other institutions clamoring for solutions to problems in preserving access and equity in teacher education. One expectation is that the document will motivate others to take the road less traveled toward improving teacher education.

CONSULTANT'S NOTE #1:

OUTSIDE LOOKING IN

EDITOR'S NOTE:

> *This is the first of a series of five notes from a consultant, Jack Gant, who worked with the Grambling College of Education in improving its Teacher Education program. These short vignettes, placed throughout the document, are designed to provide an outsider's account of what happened at Grambling. The consultant's role and responsibilities, assessment of the problem, ongoing involvement, and evaluation of the college's achievements are highlighted in these notes. The consultant's value to Grambling's success cannot be measured by the amount of space given to these notes: rather, the intent is to show another conceptual slant and to clarify the context in which planned change took place.*

At least four times each academic year since 1980, I have boarded a plane with Grambling State University as my destination. My visits were to provide the College of Education (COE) consultant-trainer services that would advance improvement of its teacher education program. This helping relationship was initiated by the dean of the college. Beyond the dean and COE faculty members, my primary clients, I have worked over a seven-year period with faculty and administrators across the entire university.

Beginning with this introductory essay, I will dissect the change process from a consultant's unique vantage point: an outsider who was intimately involved in planning and working with the improvement program over a sustained period. The inner workings of the consultant-client relationship and the impact of this relationship on the processes of reform are dominant themes. By sharing in this way the Grambling saga of hard-won excellence, I hope to enhance understanding of what happened to halt the college's decay and place it in the mainstream of colleges producing quality teachers.

It is important to the task ahead of me that the reader have adequate stage-setting information. So this first installment of Consultant's Notes explains the significant considerations I gave to building a working relationship with Grambling, as well as the theoretical framework for my work. Subsequent notes are short, crisp translations of significant organizational operations and problems. They are intended to emphasize that a consultant-trainer should help COEs to know themselves, to make decisions, to solve problems, and to develop healthy responses to social inventions, such as competency tests for teachers.

TOWARD A CONSULTATION RELATIONSHIP

My initial negotiations with Grambling's dean of education centered around establishing a short-term, consultant-client relationship. He desired outside expertise and assistance in diagnosing the organizational needs of the COE and for building a team with the entire faculty. After settling contractual matters for these services, we consummated an informal agreement on my continued involvement in any future change efforts, but I deferred my decision to participate until I could assess the outcome of this first activity. For me, from the outside looking in, the prospect of a helping relationship with Grambling raised many serious questions about the COE and its goals. Answers to the following questions, answers which the dean alone could not provide, were needed before I could consider making a long-term commitment.

1. Would planned change to improve the teacher training program be a total organizational effort (as opposed to one department)?

2. Would central administration be concerned and supportive?

3. What would be the environmental pressures for improvement?

4. Was the dean committed to change? Was the faculty committed?

5. Did the COE have any vision of its desired future state?

6. Did the COE know where it wanted to start?

7. Was there a willingness to engage in long-term consultation?

Diagnosis of the needs of the COE and the teacher education program began with a one-day retreat. Assisted by two other external consultants, I not only met the terms of the contract for this first session, but also tested the questions related to my continued involvement during this activity.

It appeared that Grambling was under much external pressure to improve the academic performance of its teaching majors, especially their performance on the National Teacher Examinations (NTE). The response to this pressure was not functional but it was there. The pervasive initial response from the faculty was that "somebody is doing something to us." Though unfocused, there was, nonetheless, obvious internal commitment–a desire on the part of the faculty to improve its program. The faculty also had definite ideas about where improvement should begin. In addition, I had some evidence that the support of central administration was there, that the president and vice president wanted to have good press and a good program. They wanted the students to pass the NTE.

On this same visit, I also observed the willingness of a small core of faculty members to lead and to work hard. The group's motivation seemed to emanate from unbridled faith in the organization's ability to regain what it had lost in image and quality. Together these factors suggested to me that the chances for Grambling's success were promising. I accepted the long-term challenge to work with the college.

As part of our contractual arrangements, I agreed to visit the campus when necessary and to work with administrators and faculty members. We further agreed that I would do some "shadow consulting." That is, I would (1) consult by phone when people had ideas or decisions to try out on me, and (2) read and react to documents that were sent to me by mail. It was also clear that the decisions would be the organization's decisions and that I would assist in examining alternatives and making recommendations. The COE, however, would have to take full responsibility for its decisions. It was clear that I would be coming in as a facilitator of problem-solving and of the COE's learning of new ways to work.

THEORETICAL INFLUENCES ON THE CONSULTANT'S APPROACH

When I entered the relationship with Grambling, I held some definite notions about historically Black teacher training colleges and their problems with teacher competency testing. I also had a relatively well-developed theory about the organizational nature of colleges of education. These conceptual tools were supplemented by a third set of theories on educational change. Given Grambling's dilemma, all three tools seemed to be appropriate; they provided general rules and guidelines for carrying out my organizational development responsibilities. By organizational development, I mean the systemwide application of behavioral science knowledge to the planned development and reinforcement of organizational strategies, structures, and processes for improving an organization's effectiveness with management from the top (Huse, 1980; French and Bell, 1978). This is not to suggest that I attempted to peddle a set of preconceived solutions to Grambling. On the contrary, my tools were heuristic devices–perceptual glasses through which to view, size up and help the college improve its effectiveness.

The works of Lewin and Beckhard greatly influenced my consultative approach from a research perspective. Lewin suggested three steps to bring about change in an organization: unfreeze the organization, make the necessary transformations, then refreeze the organization so that new transformations are a part of the natural state of things. Beckhard, on the other hand, suggested that change agents look early at the organization's desired future state of existence, and at its present state for transitional points where intervention will be possible while simultaneously gaining the commitment to change.

CRITICAL ORGANIZATIONAL CHARACTERISTICS OF GRAMBLING

Grambling had what seemed to be some unique characteristics that influenced my approach to working with the COE. I observed these during my first visit to the campus. The most distinctive of these features follow.

- The university seemed to operate on the assumption that it was first an institution of higher education. Being historically Black was a legacy and a secondary factor that was quickly becoming a misnomer. The growing international populations of faculty and students signaled this change.

- At the executive level, a primary operating norm was to not make excuses for the often low-entry skills and poor performance of students. For example, the attitude was that if other students could pass competency tests, then Grambling's students could too–and would. Therefore, on the matter of competency testing for teachers, central administration was more disturbed about what the institution had not done than by what it had done that simply had not worked.

- Grambling's survival strategy, in part (a large part at that) appeared to operationalize survival as a process of meeting the challenges of the system rather than fighting it; respecting the system, but not fearing it; negotiating the system instead of running from it; and challenging the system, when necessary, from a proactive posture rather than waiting on the system to force it into a reactive posture. Thus, Grambling was far from being a passive organization.

UNIQUE DIMENSIONS OF THE PROBLEM

Tests of my working tools during the faculty retreat gave me more than preliminary knowledge about the existing motivational levels, leadership styles, individual temperaments, and the nature of different organizational groups. Analyses of the diagnostic data collected by the consulting team pointed up three unique dimensions of the problem. First, the issue of boundary in Grambling's teacher education program was unclear. Did teacher education take place in units other than the College of Education? If so, what was the dean's job–just dean of the College of Education with no authority and responsibility outside the unit in matters pertaining to education majors, or also director of the system of teacher education with authority and responsibility for leadership in all matters (inside and outside the COE) affecting education majors?

Second, there seemed to be no common guiding principles, operating procedures, and coordinated policies and procedures concerning the teacher education system. After some engagement and discussions, the following principles and assumptions were agreed upon.

1. In public education, curriculum belongs to the public. The legislature represents the public and sets minimum standards for licensure.

2. The NTE, which is professionally developed, represents the minimum curriculum for teacher education in Louisiana and several other states.

3. Students have a right to be taught that on which they will be tested for licensure.

4. Courses represent the primary unit for the delivery of knowledge. Courses should be assigned NTE competencies that should be included in course syllabi, made public to students and faculty, taught using appropriate instructional techniques, and monitored.

5. Courses belong to departments and institutions, not to professors. Departments decide what; professors decide how.

6. System goals are most achievable when inputs, transformations, and outputs are set by faculty and administrators.

7. Rewards must be commensurate with work in the system's culture.

Underlying Grambling's new philosophy was the newly sanctioned position of the COE dean as director of the system of teacher education at the university.

Third, application of Beckhard's theory for identifying all possible intervention points within the organization produced a substantial list of target areas for reform in Grambling's COE: admissions, recruitment, resources, advisement, curriculum, instruction, orientation, and students. However, the college did not have the luxury of looking at these targets as possible entry points. Survival of the college demanded that each identified problem area be a number-one priority. This finding suggested a multiple intervention strategy. The term "shotgun approach" was used by leadership. This approach supported the change-theory concept that changes in any subsystem require changes in other parts of the system.

CHAPTER 2

LITERACY IN STUDENT PERFORMANCE: A DATA BASE FOR CHANGE

The value of research to effective academic practice is well understood by Gramblinites institutionwide. Beginning in 1980, the College of Education increasingly conducted, translated, and consumed its own research to understand the academic performance of its preservice teachers. New information was sought to support program planning and evaluation of the college's improvement efforts. Assessment of the research program indicates that it was crucial to the positive outcomes of the college's improvement efforts in all areas. The research program has evolved into a self-perpetuating data base, keeping the college current and literate about changes in its students' performance. Research now serves as the primary tool for tracking and solving problems as the college institutionalizes its new program.

WHAT TYPE OF LITERACY?

Research studies initiated in 1980 were a natural extension of a few earlier studies conducted by different people at the university. Individual and group performance of education majors on the NTE and comparison of Grambling's NTE scores with those of other state institutions were the major issues in these earlier investigations. Subsequently, the College's expanded research objective demanded answers to the following questions:

- What are the characteristics (academic history, ACT scores, major field of study, etc.) of preservice teachers who pass the NTE on the first try?

- How proficient are preservice teacher education majors in the basic skills areas?

- How do preservice teachers compare on the NTE by certification areas?

- What, if anything, are other colleges and departments on campus doing to help preservice teachers in their academic disciplines to pass the NTE?

- To what extent are faculty universitywide aware of the NTE's content and structure?

- What type of NTE test items give our preservice teachers the most trouble?

- Is there a correlation between performance on the ACT and NTE? Should a specific ACT score be required for entrance into teacher education?

- At which points in their academic careers should preservice teachers take certain parts of the NTE? Should preservice teachers take the entire examination on the same day?

- Is there a correlation between grades and NTE scores of preservice teachers?

- What are other Louisiana institutions doing to prepare teaching majors for the NTE? What are the entrance, retention, and exit competency assessment requirements at other Louisiana institutions?

- How do students feel about the NTE after taking it? Before taking it?

Answers to these questions were not obtained with "quick and dirty" techniques. While some studies were one-time inquiries and less complex than others, nevertheless, they were systematically approached as meaningful scientific undertakings. Other studies were longitudinal investigations yielding intermittent findings and remaining in progress even today. Most current research is conducted by the college's Center for Field Services and Research, but initially the expanded research program was conducted by anyone assigned or with personal interest in a research task, usually faculty members with demonstrated research and evaluation skills.

THE PAINS OF LITERACY: SIGNIFICANT RESEARCH FINDINGS

What did the research findings reveal about Grambling's teacher education majors? In general, the findings confirmed that intervention strategies before 1980 (mainly the short-term study sessions and the NTE awareness course) were ineffective. Trend data on the failure rate of students stood in evidence. A sample of these data is displayed in Table 4.

Table 4

RESULTS OF NATIONAL TEACHER EXAMINATIONS
GRAMBLING STATE UNIVERSITY
COLLEGE OF EDUCATION
1978-1980

	1978	1979			1980		
	Dec	May	Aug	Dec	May	Aug	Dec
Number completing a teacher Education Program	69	69	29	64	65	19	51
Number of the above who took the NTE	69	58	29	64	65	19	36
Number of the above who attained the appropriate score	0	2(3%)	3(10%)	2(3%)	4(6%)	3(15%)	10(27%)
Number of the above who were certifiable	*7(10%)	7(12%)	5(17%)	9(14%)	10(15%)	5(26%)	16(44%)
Number of the above non-certifiable (Did not attain appropriate score)	69	56	26	62	61	16	26

Follow-up studies of majors between 1978 and 1980 revealed little difference even in the scores of students who took the test a second time. For example, of the 108 students who sat for the NTE in December 1978, 69 were enrolled students or recent graduates. Of this number, 34 (49%) were taking the test a second time for initial certification. Of the 34 repeaters only two (6%) fully satisfied certification criteria, 94 percent failed. Table 5 contains a statistical summary of these findings.

---

* These candidates were able to acquire provisional licensure because their scores were within 10% of the requirement.

Table 5
1978-1979 Report of Students Who Repeated the National Teacher Examination

Academic Majors Group	# Taking Test	Common Examination Test Scores			# Taking Test	Area Examination Test Scores		
		1st Test Date 11/78	2nd Test Date 07/79	Difference in Test Scores		1st Test Date 11/78	2nd Test Date 02/79	Difference in Test Scores
Total	34							
Lowest		302	330	28				
Highest		526	526	70				
Mean		426	414	12				
Elem. Ed.	18				18			
Lowest		339	287	52		360	420	+60
Highest		511	596	85		540	600	+60
Mean		430	426	4		456	490	+34
ECE	5							
Lowest		302	284	18		340	270	70
Highest		449	414	35		480	510	+30
Mean		378	367	11		424	370	54
Biol. Ed.	1							
Lowest		509	525	16				
Highest		509	525	16				
Mean		509	525	16				
Math Ed.	1				1			
Lowest		477	425	52		440	440	0
Highest		477	425	52		440	440	0
Mean		477	425	52		440	440	0
Soc. Sci. Ed.	1				1			
Lowest		526	491	35		480	540	+60
Highest		526	491	35		480	540	+60
Mean		526	491	35		480	540	+60
Phy. Ed.	3				3			
Lowest		354	334	20		440	430	10
Highest		474	428	46		500	480	20
Mean		417	367	50		470	463	7
Music Ed.	2				3			
Lowest		445	428	17		400	370	30
Highest		530	512	18		530	530	0
Mean		488	470	18		465	450	15
French Ed.	1				1			
Lowest		415	429	14		415	429	+14
Highest		415	429	14		415	429	+14
Mean		415	429	14		415	429	+14
Ed. of Ment. Ret.	2				2			
Lowest		335	330	5		370	390	+20
Highest		372	355	17		430	440	+10
Mean		354	343	11		400	415	+15

Further analyses of repeat testing performance on common and area examination suggest other trends. In most instances mean scores on the NTE commons examination decreased at second testings, but scores on area examinations tended overall to increase slightly. An obvious implication from the data is that prior short-term coaching failed to have lasting impact on learning. Another implication is that little student preparation for taking the test a second time had occurred. Such preparation would need to have been student initiated since most second timers were graduates. Analysis of 1980 and 1981 data produced similar findings. Finally, in 1982 significant differences were found between the first and second efforts of preservice teachers to pass the NTE.

Seeking to learn why Grambling's preservice teachers were failing repeatedly to show progress, the college brought in a number of consultants to assist in analyzing student performance. One of these consultants suggested that reading proficiency may not have been the only problem, but it certainly appeared to be a significant part of the problem. This observation eventually led to a 1981-1982 study of the basic skills abilities of preservice teachers in four areas: reading, writing, mathematics, and English.

A randomly selected sample of 33 sophomore, junior, and senior students were administered (a) the Nelson-Denny Reading Test for vocabulary and comprehension; (b) a college-developed essay instrument for syntax, semantics, spelling, punctuation, and sentence structure measures; (c) the Sequential Test of Educational Progress (STEP) in mathematics and English for computation, basic math concepts, and usage of standard English measures; and (d) the ACT for additional measures in a variety of areas.

Findings from these test batteries were devastating to faculty and administrators. Summaries of student performance on these tests appear in Tables 6, 7, and 8. Resulting composite student profiles are presented in Table 9.

Table 6

A SUMMARY OF NELSON-DENNY TEST SCORES

VOCABULARLY		COMPREHENSION		COMPOSITE		%RANK	
GRADE LEVEL	# OF STUDENTS	GRADE LEVEL	# OF STUDENTS	GRADE LEVEL	# OF STUDENTS	%	# OF STUDENTS
15.0	1	14.6	1	14.1	1		
14.6	1	13.5	1	13.9	1	33	1
14.5	1	13.2	4	13.8	1	28	1
14.2	1	12.8	1	13.4	1	27	1
13.6	1	12.2	3	13.3	1	21	2
13.5	1	11.5	2	12.7	1	19	1
12.4	1	10.8	2	12.6	1	12	1
12.0	1	10.0	1	12.3	1	11	1
11.1	2	9.3	1	11.6	1	10	1
10.9	2	8.7	4	11.3	2	8	1
9.2	3	8.1	1	10.4	1	7	2
8.9	3	7.7	1	10.0	3	5	1
8.6	2	7.5	3	9.8	1	4	1
8.3	3	7.0	4	8.9	1	3	4
8.1	2	6.6	2	8.5	1	2	1
7.9	2	6.3	1	8.3	2	1	13
7.7	2			8.1	1		
7.5	3			7.9	1		
				7.7	2		
				7.5	1		
				7.1	2		
				6.9	1		
				6.6	2		
				6.2	1		
Mean 10.3		**9.8**		**9.9**			

%=Percentile

Table 7

RESULTS FROM WRITING TEST

WRITING LEVEL		NUMBER OF ERRORS	
Grade Level	# of Students	Errors	Students
12.0	1	25	1
11.0	1	21	1
10.0	2	20	1
9.0	2	19	1
8.0	1	18	1
7.5	1	17	1
7.0	11	15	1
6.0	3	14	2
5.0	2	13	2
4.0	0	11	1
BN	5	10	2
		9	2
		8	2
		7	4
		6	1
		5	5
		3	1
Mean 7.5		12.4	

BN=Below Norms

Table 8

RESULTS FROM STEP AND ACT

STEP MATHEMATICS % RANK		STEP ENGLISH %RANK		ACT (COMP)	
% RANK	# OF STUDENTS	% RANK	# OF STUDENT	SCORE	# OF STUDENTS
50	1	59	1	19	1
41	3	53	1	18	1
36	1	47	3	14	1
26	3	43	1	13	3
23	2	36	1	12	3
20	1	28	2	11	4
13	1	25	2	10	2
10	1	21	2	9	3
7	3	13	1	8	5
5	1	11	4	7	3
4	2	8	2	6	2
2	1	7	1		
1	3	5	1		

Mean - 10.2
COE

Mean - 11.1
University

% =Percentile

Table 9
COMPOSITE STUDENT PROFILES

	NELSON-DENNY					WRITING		STEP		ACT
STUD.#	VOC.	COMPRE-HENSION	TOTAL	RATE	% Rank	WRITING LEVEL	ERRORS	MATH. HIGH-SCHOOL	ENG. HIGH-SCHOOL	COMPOSITE
1	7.7	7.5	7.1	6.5	1%	7.0	8			8
2	11.1	12.2	11.6	14.6	8%	11.0	5	10%	47%	
3	15.+	12.2	14.1	None	33%	BN	10	26%	47%	
4	9.2	8.7	8.9	11.3	2%	7.0	21	4%	11%	9
5	8.3	8.7	8.5	BN	1%	7.0	17			
6	7.5	8.7	7.7	7.0	1%	BN	5	1%	6%	
7	14.6	13.2	13.9	6.0	28%					
8	8.1	7.5	7.5	BN	1%	5.0	4	7%	25%	7
9	14.2	14.6	13.4	BN	21%	12.0	7			11
10	14.2	12.2	13.3	6.5	19%	BN	14	50%	43%	19
11	8.6	11.5	10.0	BN	3%	7.0	9	13%	13%	9
12	11.1	13.2	12.3	10.3	10%	6.0	3			
13	8.9	7.5	8.1	9.1	1%	7.0	5	23%	21%	
14	12.0	8.1	10.0	8.4	3%	10.0	13	5%	47%	
15	7.9	7.0	6.9	None	1%	7.0	9			8
16	10.9	10.0	10.4	8.4	4%	6.0	7	7%	25%	8
17	8.1	8.7	8.3	8.4	1%	5.0	19	23%	7%	
18	12.9	9.3	11.3	7.7	7%	11.0	6	41%	59%	13
19	13.5	11.5	12.7	7.7	12%	7.0	7			
20	14.5	13.2	13.8	14.6	28%	6.0	14			18
21	7.5	6.6	6.2	6.0	1%	7.0	6	20%	11%	11
22	8.6	10.0	9.8	12.3	3%	BN	10			
23	8.9	7.0	7.7	BN	1%	BN	18			
24	9.2	10.8	10.0	10.3	3%	9.0	8	26%	28%	11
25	10.0	7.0	8.3	6.0	1%	7.5	10			
26	7.7	7.7	7.1	BN	1%	7.0	25			9
27	9.2	7.0	7.9	AN	21%	8.0	5	2%	53%	
28	8.9	13.2	11.3	11.3	7%	10.0	8	41%	28%	14
29	8.3	10.8	9.5	AN	2%	6.0	20			
30	13.6	13.5	13.4	AN	28%	9.0	5	41%	36%	
31	12.4	12.8	12.6	6.5	11%	7.0	9			8
32	8.3	6.3	6.6	AN	1%	7.0	15	7%	8%	
33	7.9	6.6	6.6	8.4	1%	4.0	11	36%	5%	6

*BN=Below Norms
**AN=Above Norms
%=Percentile

Reading Performance. The sample performed across a wide range of grade levels, from 7.5 to 15.0+. Seventeen (52%) of the students demonstrated vocabulary proficiency at the seventh and eighth grade levels. Comprehension scores also covered a wide range, with the lowest score at the sixth grade level, the highest at grade 14.6, and a mean score at ninth grade level. Almost half of these students scored below the eighth grade in comprehension and in composite reading scores.

Writing Performance. According to one member of the two-person research team, "Writing level was assessed by having students write a passage of at least 100 words on a subject of the students' choice." Each passage was then evaluated by four qualified persons and the errors in syntax, semantics, spelling, punctuation, and sentence structure were marked. Errors were categorized for individual students at a later date. The fewest number of errors on any passage was three and the highest number was 25. The mean number of errors was 12.4. For the most part, students seemed to make more errors in punctuating with commas than in any other area of writing. Misspelled words, run-on sentences, sentence fragments, and improper use of inflectional endings also were frequent mistakes. One researcher advised that five students' writing scores were below the norms and immeasurable. No student was estimated to be writing at the college level.

Mathematics and English Performance. Mathematics percentile scores echoed reading and writing outcomes. Of the 23 scores considered, only one student scored at the 50th percentile. All others scored below this rank. On the English portion of the STEP test, percentile ranks ranged from five to 59. For these same preservice teachers, the mean ACT score was 10.2 compared to 11.1 for students universitywide.

Other studies presented equally insightful and painful findings about the test performance of Grambling's preservice teachers. Space limitations, however, disallow statistical illuminations of the data in this document. Summative statements from investigative findings only are presented next.

- No significant positive relationship was found between the ACT and NTE scores of preservice teachers.

- Generally, preservice teachers felt that all students should be required to take more tests and should learn to appreciate the importance of tests.

- Preservice teachers seldom completed standardized tests, (including the NTE), in the time allotted by testing regulations.

- Preservice teachers who took the NTE at or after graduation felt they had forgotten the humanities and history information taught during their freshman and sophomore years.

- Except for 1978, between 1976 to 1980 preservice teachers scored lower on the professional education portion of the NTE commons examination than they did in any other area.

- Faculty-developed tests and classroom activities prior to 1982 conditioned students to use and reinforce their use of lower-order thinking skills; the NTE frequently required more complex levels of thinking.

- Few, if any, faculty-developed tests before 1982 contained items in the format of the NTE.

Multiple research-based information increased literacy about the problem of student performance among faculty across the entire campus. As literacy increased, other academic units increased their cooperation in problem solving with the College of Education. Most of all, research findings helped reduce the aura of complexity that first tended to obscure the faculty's vision of alternatives for achieving excellence. In fact, the data often dictated the college's next steps.

IMPLICATIONS FOR ACTION: ACCEPTANCE AND ACCOMMODATION

Findings about preservice teachers' basic-skills performance, professional knowledge, and testing sophistication argued for massive curricular revision, faculty development, and faculty accountability. Also, the findings further substantiated reality: The College of Education was being blamed in toto for poor student performance, including performance in general education. Although true sentiments in the college were typified by chagrin and indignation at having to assume a precarious position of leading institutional reform, it seemed necessary to do so. After all, the real issue was survival–explicitly for the college and its faculty, and implicitly for Black teachers, historically Black institutions, and Black cultural heritage. Survival necessarily rested upon improving total student performance.

ACCEPTING EXPANDED ROLES AND RESPONSIBILITIES

Despite rigidly perceived lines of demarcation between the expertise found in colleges of education and in colleges of arts and sciences, College of Education faculty members tend to be academic hybrids. They are prepared in both subject matter disciplines and the professional education of teachers. Nevertheless, once in a college of education, these hybrids usually come to perceive their roles and

33

responsibilities as unidimensional: preparing teachers in the professional methods and techniques of teaching. Pedagogy and methodology become their prized work areas; courses in general studies typically are viewed as some other unit's territory.

Prompted by research findings, faculty members in Grambling's College of Education discovered they could no longer afford such a stringent division of labor and fragmented treatment of students. They had to assume some responsibility for remediation and they had to incorporate a basic-skills curriculum (especially in reading and communicative skills) into professional academic courses. In other words, education faculty members had to have an impact on the total education of preservice teachers. Traditional fragmentation of the teacher education program would continue to leave the college's fate too much to chance. This responsibility was an obscure dimension of excellence, a different challenge from what was first perceived by faculty members. Faculty roles and responsibilities would have to be redefined to address all observed deficiencies and to demonstrate meaningful acceptance of the challenge of excellence.

Research evidence also supported the need for an aggressive marketing campaign to sell ownership in the problem of student performance. To the extent that faculty members outside the College of Education could be influenced to improve their own program weaknesses, a return in the future to a more equitable workload for teacher education was probable. Until then, several enabling objectives for influencing faculty acceptance demanded attention. The College of Education had to

1. identify new roles for its faculty members (e.g., who had studied math, English, etc.?).

2. help its faculty understand the nature of their new roles and responsibilities (e.g., basic skills plus professional education).

3. guide its faculty in successfully assuming new roles and responsibilities (e.g., revising courses, remediating students, developing curricula).

Expansion of the college's role and mission in teacher education commenced with actions to influence faculty acceptance of the idea. These actions were not an attempt to undermine other academic programs at the university; nor were they a misinterpretation of collected data. Research findings emphasized the need for extra effort by all academic units. As part of its leadership role in teacher education, the College of Education took the initiative in giving this extra effort.

ACCOMMODATING EXPANDED ROLES AND RESPONSIBILITIES

The college's next step was to determine what implications research findings held for operationalizing the accepted, expanded training mission of the college. Faculty members in the College of Education raised numerous questions in their effort to understand the college's new position and to understand what was expected of them. Would the college subordinate professional education to general education? Would the college lower its academic standards? What form should intervention strategies for remediation take? How should these new experiences be incorporated into the existing schedules of the college? The faculty? The students? Where would new teaching materials come from for remediation?

As faculty and students learned later, subordinating knowledge of any kind and lowering academic standards were far from the minds of change agents in the college. The teacher education program was revised and expanded to accommodate all new experiences. Expansion, drawing upon research findings, included rearranging physical space by literally knocking down walls, consolidating some resources while creating others, hiring new personnel to fill gaps in available expertise, fighting accompanying political battles, and implementing reform wherever there was a need.

Accommodation was not an easy task. It cost the college in several areas. First, there was the cost of time commitment. Time was needed for staff development sessions, development of course outlines and examinations, and preparation and dissemination of student progress reports. Planning periods and time previously given to faculty meetings was needed for staff development sessions and follow-up activities. Second, the expanded role cost faculty members their comfort with cherished traditions. Time to think about and test out the new behaviors they exchanged for old and familiar behaviors was minimal. This pressure left many faculty members feeling anxious and uncertain about what they were doing. Third, there was an exorbitant cost in physical stamina. Work required energy, staff development required attendance, creative materials development required thinking, and increased interactions with students required being visible and available most of the time.

Acceptance and accommodation activities represent decisions based upon sound facts and reasoning. There remains little to be explained about acceptance of the college's expanded role and mission, but much is left to be shared about the intricacies of accommodating students' academic needs.

CONSULTANT'S NOTE #2:

THE CHANGE ENVIRONMENT

Change does not occur in a vacuum. Change also affects and is affected by the environment in which the system operates. Of course, the closer the ties are between the organization and its environment, the more impact the actions of one will have on the other. It is easy for an organization that has evolved into a near-closed system to forget about the impact the environment can have upon the system's change efforts. In effect, the external environment may be likened to a foundation with many cracks and crannies. If left unplugged or untreated, the cracks grow wider, the crannies grow deeper and the foundation, eventually just erodes away. Thus sponsors of change must attend to a multiplicity of significant forces in the environment, in addition to the forces it creates for itself. They must (a) prepare these forces for change, (b) influence ownership in the problem, (c) seek input in the development of alternative solutions, (d) obtain from them commitment to support change efforts, and (e) generate involvement in the implementation of a change strategy.

The COE perceived preparing the Grambling campus for change and influencing other academic units to accept some responsibility for the performance of students as its greatest challenges. This perception turned out to be somewhat exaggerated. My guess is that there are two reasons that preparing and influencing the campus to support the COE was less difficult than anticipated. The first reason has to do with the maternalistic stance of the university. The second reason centers upon how the COE used my services as an external consultant when it first began to deal with this matter. These two reasons are addressed in the remaining entries of this note.

MATERNALISTIC SUPPORT OF THE COE

One of the most impressive things about my work with Grambling was experiencing Grambling itself. Institutional pride, anxiety over the school's problems and negative public image, determination to survive and a special tenderness toward the COE, all feelings that are seldom clearly visible at some institutions, were readily apparent on this campus. The COE seemed to hold much meaning for the entire university. This was unusual in a period when many institutions of higher education, confronted by colossal problems in enrollments and economic stability, seemed quite willing to offer colleges of education as sacrificial lambs. Grambling was not so inclined. Its COE was perceived as the fountainhead of the university. As such, the populace evidenced in 1980 signs of pain and despondency over the student performance problems of this font; paradoxically, these same people exhibited a widespread undercurrent of hope and an unusual tolerant attitude.

Only hairline cracks were observable in the maternalistic support relationship between the COE and its academic support units across campus. Observation suggested that (a) the COE had not communicated its problems well to others on campus, (b) support units had inadequate data on those aspects of student performance that reflected their involvement, (c) support units had never received a direct appeal for substantive assistance, and (d) support units were operating on the same misperceptions of the role of the dean and programming in teacher education as faculty in the COE. My assessment of the situation was that these cracks had to be plugged. Some of these outside forces had to be worked on.

PLUGGING CRACKS IN THE COE'S SUPPORT RELATIONSHIPS

One support relationship was the group of deans and department heads who influenced general education and those teacher education units that were outside the COE. They had to be made a part of the effort. We decided to begin with the COE dean calling the group together. Our goal was to be working in the future from a position of power and authority. Two things from this meeting were needed to give us this position: program approval and support from these top people. We also desired their support of the fact that teacher education was, indeed, a total university effort.

Our approach was for me to facilitate an issue-clarification and commitment-building session, with only university deans and department heads present. The COE dean was just another member of the group. We began the session on the premise that this was part of doing our job for students, and it was students who would come out ahead. Establishing this professional outlook was critical, I feel, to the successful outcomes of the session. If we had presented our agenda as a power play, we probably would have generated a different response. Commitment planning generally succeeds best when the significant others are treated with respect and are involved in planning and changes that may affect them.

Because it was necessary for members of the group to view themselves as being in teacher education with the COE dean as director, irrespective of where they were structurally, we worked through with this group the same set of principles and assumptions agreed upon by the COE previously (See Note #1). The deans and department heads had few problems with these issues. In the end they also supported them. They understood their roles. Moreover they wanted to be able to maintain their pride in the institution, and they wanted students to share this pride. So theoretically and structurally, teacher education now had its leader. That leadership was not only for the COE, but the boundaries had been expanded so that the other units felt structurally included in the teacher education system. These significant others seemed to have realized and accepted the fact that the president had appointed the dean of education as the director of all teacher education on campus.

In response to the data presented, the group concluded, like the COE faculty, that a "shotgun approach" to the problem was needed; interventions would have to be made in all areas. More importantly, members of the group committed themselves to making these interventions under the dean's leadership. There were few other cracks and crannies in environmental relationships that the COE could not handle. Nevertheless, we monitored its activities in these areas. From time-to-time I was queried for my perceptions, which I freely gave, on certain matters. The major structural understandings and commitment planning for forces within the teacher education system were now in place.

CHAPTER 3

FIRST THINGS FIRST:
PREPARATION FOR CHANGE

The enigma of "first things first" in Grambling's case was in determining a reference point for importance–important to whom and for what reason? Improving students' scores on the NTE was top priority; this was the most vexing problem, one needing immediate redress. The goal of excellence would in all likelihood necessitate massive reform over an extended period of time–more time than the college had to affect immediate NTE outcomes.

So the college's first energies were channeled into two existing bandage activities–the Advanced Test Awareness Seminar and special NTE study sessions–until a more permanent strategy could be implemented. Both activities were designed in 1980 to address issues related to attendance, content, format, and study materials. Some of these issues surfaced during reviews of college records. Interviews with faculty members who had been responsible for the seminar and special sessions disclosed other issues. Once the college's bandages were properly applied, attention refocused on developing a model teacher preparation program.

Reviews of Grambling's 1980 faculty-needs-assessment data showed that extensive preparation for turning the college around transpired. Awareness of the problems had been instigated by research and related staff development and by external means such as newspaper reports. The real chore now was helping individual faculty members, administrators and students understand how they contributed to the problem and what they could do to bring about its solution. It was a matter of selling change.

SELLING OWNERSHIP IN CHANGE

The college's selling job began with adoption of the theory, "people are most willing to change those things which they identify for themselves as needing to be changed." Administrators and the college's consultant seemed to think that this could best be achieved by presenting people with raw data about their performance. Such an approach had to be finite and public to be effective, they advised internal change agents, thereby eliminating hiding places for faculty members and causing them to confront the consequences of individual behavior.

On this theory, an aggressive campaign to sell ownership in the problem of improving student performance commenced. Marketing information and ideas transcended the College of Education. Believing student performance to be a university responsibility, the College of Education invited and central administration supported participation by other colleges in all improvement activities from the outset. Although participation by outside units evolved slowly, it increased eventually to a respectable level.

As part of the marketing strategy, findings about student performance on the NTE were reduced to palatable reports for examination by all university faculty members and administrators. There were reports for each academic area (math, science, English, professional education, etc.). There were reports by academic majors. There were reports which compared the performance of some majors to that of other majors, and there were reports of student performance trends over the preceding five years.

Data sources varied. "In house" data sources about teacher education majors included NTE score reports on students who passed and students who failed the NTE; an item analysis of scores from the November, 1978 test date (from ETS); a summary analysis of STEP Test Results for Spring 1980; The Staff Development Report, September 1980; an informal study of Grambling's existing efforts to improve NTE scores; interviews with students who were presently enrolled in the Advanced Test Awareness Seminar; and various survey findings of faculty perceptions and behaviors. The new research undertakings reported in Chapter 2 later offered an additional data source.

To supplement in-house data sources, consultants from Educational Testing Services (ETS), producer of the NTE, were brought to campus. They shared student performance data that confirmed the College's findings. Data from ETS, however, was in one sense more finite than the college's data. Even the percentage of students who answered each question correctly was made available for review. This information was invaluable. It held direct implications for what was being taught or what was supposed to be taught in individual courses. Many faculty members who taught related courses often attended these special sessions. Most of those in attendance quickly realized that indirectly their instructional behaviors were under scrutiny along with student performance.

As with any worthwhile marketing plan, follow-up activities for helping faculty members to internalize and to interpret the need for change transpired. Always these activities were designed either to review existing data or to generate data for planning. Sessions were conducted primarily using three formats: universitywide information sessions; college and universitywide workshops; and small group meetings for brainstorming, goal setting, and problem solving. Session agenda items frequently included: (a) analyzing NTE competencies and course competencies to determine how and where the two matched, (b) analyzing examination copies of the NTE for both content and structure, (c) comparing the structure of NTE questions with the structure of faculty-developed tests, and

(d) conducting additional assessments of faculty and students to fill gaps in the college's information base. Findings from all survey data were made public. However, information on students in the form of student profiles was sent initially to department heads and students' advisors. Later the profiles were sent to persons responsible for remediation services to students.

Another important follow-up activity was having individual departments in the College of Education to review department-specific data on student performance. Departmental reviews usually followed large group sessions. Reviews were designed to culminate in goal setting, with development of related measurable objectives for both the department and individual members of the department. These departmental planning products were then submitted to the dean of education for approval and dissemination for collegewide consumption. How progress on achieving objectives was monitored is addressed in a later chapter. Disseminating special reports beyond the College of Education, conducting surveys, exchanging ideas with other institutions, and collecting and displaying student development materials were among the college's other activities.

Selling ownership in change did not transpire in isolation from other college thrusts. Believing linear action to be an unaffordable luxury, concurrent improvements were launched in areas considered equally critical to preparing for change. One such thrust centered on academic standards for both students and faculty.

SETTING NEW ACADEMIC STANDARDS FOR STUDENT PERFORMANCE

That students lacked ability to perform adequately was never the belief of faculty members in the College of Education. That students were not challenged, did not have prerequisite skills, and lacked self-confidence was the belief of most faculty members. Among the supporting observations of faculty members are these shared perceptions about student performance:

> Students are not coming to classes as they should; and, if they come they are usually late.

> ****

> Our students don't become serious about their studies until

41

their junior and senior years. It's too late then.

****

They find time to do everything else but attend special study sessions. And since they know they're not required to take the test awareness course, they will not register for it.

****

When our students come from general studies they bring *A's* and *B's*, but their classroom performance does not validate these grades. Many of them cannot read or write a decent sentence. We allow them into our advanced courses, but how can we expect them to perform at an advanced level, when they can't do the basics?

From this perspective, college administrators and the faculty defined the problem of student performance as the college's failure to set appropriate academic standards consistent with emerging needs, to enforce those which already existed, and to abolish standards rendered inappropriate by time and change. Further they contended, if in the future new standards were not set and enforced, students would continue to perform below acceptable levels.

What actions did the college take? A simplistic response is that it set new academic standards and devised a monitoring system to enforce them. Implementing this strategy was not a simplistic process. It required the following steps:

1. Studying existing university and college level policies and seeking changes in those that failed to support acceptable academic performance (e.g., class attendance).

2. Observing instructor's behavior in conducting classes (e.g., starting classes on time, keeping accurate attendance records), and reaching consensus on new behavior.

3. Diagnosing the basic skills students need on entering teacher education, comparing needs with grades and curricula of other departments to determine the source of discrepancies, and working with other units to increase their standards. (The College found that many students were unable to read at the 12th grade level but were being released from developmental studies because of insufficient personnel to handle the large number of student clients. The standard for passing reading was at the 8th grade level; the readability level of the average college text is at the 12th and 13th grade levels.)

4. Setting new admission standards and procedures for entry into the college, a department, a program, and certain key courses (explained in detail in Chapter 7).

5. Requiring students who were given conditional-admission status to show evidence of having successfully met stipulated conditions (i.e., remediation experiences) before being fully admitted or moving to the next admission step.

6. Installing NTE-like departmental examinations and requiring students to take components of the actual examination at specified points in their academic careers.

7. Increasing the writing and thinking requirements of courses.

Newly developed standards were incorporated gradually into college operations. Students were introduced to these new standards, related requirements, and revised procedures each academic term as changes were made. Faculty and students were given notice of the dates new requirements were to become effective, thus providing time for practice and preparation. To no one's surprise, with the formalization of each new requirement, the college had to engage in show-and-tell exercises–that is, **SHOW** students and faculty they could not avoid meeting the requirements, and **TELL** them again the requirements they failed to meet.

A significant observation about the implementation of new standards for students is that: every new standard and set of actions for students meant reciprocal standards and actions (equal to or more demanding than those required of students) for faculty members and administrators. For example, the new admission standards required faculty advisors to keep more accurate records, to have increased contact with advisees, and to evaluate records in greater depth than they had in the past. It also meant learning a multi-step, cumbersome procedure (before its refinement), and explaining this procedure to students.

It took faculty members quite a while to adjust to these new demands on their time. Remonstrative complaints from some of them, followed by avoidance behavior, led to a crisis in advisement that threatened to block goal achievement. Student development focusing on advisement, refinement of the admissions process, and subsequent reorganization of the college deflected the block.

PREPARING THE CHANGE ENVIRONMENT

Environment is both a determinant and a target of change. At least Grambling envisioned it as such. Hence the deduction: If the environment improves, then instruction will improve; and, if instruction improves, then student performance will improve. However, a plethora of definitions for environment existed within the college. Understanding these definitions is requisite to understanding the college's actions to prepare the environment for change.

At its most fundamental level, environment to faculty meant more teaching supplies and support services. To students it meant being able to see advisors when they needed them, being treated courteously by staff and faculty members, and graduating on schedule. To administrators though, environment meant all of these things and more.

First, administrators saw Grambling's change environment as extending beyond the university campus. It existed in the minds of legislators and parish-level school administrators; it existed with whatever or whomever had some linkage with the college. Second, they saw the entire university campus as part of the environment. Third, administrators appeared to define environment as the organization of human resources for bringing about optimum results. Preparing the environment for change meant reconditioning these areas to bring about a positive impact on the college. These viewpoints are made clearer in the ensuing discussion.

TEACHING SUPPLIES AND SUPPORT SERVICES

Whether additional teaching supplies and support services are available matters little if faculty members perceive them as being unavailable. Thus, one gesture toward ensuring goal achievement is to provide what the faculty members perceive they need to do an effective job. These words were never spoken by the dean of education, but his actions, described as follows, implied this philosophical stance.

Before and during the early 1980s, the college had one copier that was obtained through a grant. Also there was one ditto machine, one small binder, one 16mm projector, two working overhead projectors, and no computers. This almost exhaustive list typified the college's other resources. With a small writing team, the dean produced several funded proposals that dramatically altered the college's resource picture. Five copiers, 10 computers, video taping equipment, a heavy-duty binder, and at least 10 memory writers were added to the equipment inventory. In addition, the amount of consumable supplies for the education faculty increased.

The idea of a preprofessional accountability laboratory was developed into a multi-unit resource center to meet the need for support services to faculty and students. Five classrooms were remodeled to house the center's computer laboratory, tutorial laboratory, media laboratory, materials development laboratory, and teaching resource center for aids and print materials. External funds were also used for the center's development.

The new resources were an additional stimulus for change. Clearly, new support services influenced the multiplication of remediation efforts, the creative development of new instructional materials, and the enhancement of faculty skills. Subsequently, as the substance and structure of learning resources changed, so did the behavior of students.

IMPROVING THE ADVISORY SYSTEM

Unlike situations at many other institutions, most faculty members in the College of Education at Grambling were responsible for advising undergraduate students. Besides helping students to plan programs of study upon entry into the college, they signed students' registration forms, documented students' academic progress, recommended students for admission, performed academic counseling, and validated students' readiness for graduation. Except for implementing new admission procedures, these responsibilities remained the same after 1980.

How advisement responsibilities were discharged beginning in 1981, however, is a key difference worthy of sharing. Changes in advisory operations included the following.

1. <u>Identifying prospective education majors and initiating advisement during the second semester of their freshmen year</u>. Previously majors were not identified nor was advisement in education begun until students' junior year. Early identification and early advisement were steps designed to (a) give students more accurate information earlier in their academic careers, (b) reduce the chances of advisement leading to ill-planned programs for students, (c) facilitate earlier identification and remediation of students' academic deficiencies, and (d) keep advisors abreast of students' total education experiences.

2. <u>Increasing collaboration among College of Education, College of Liberal Arts, and College of Science and Technology faculties in the advisement of students</u>. Second semester freshmen in the past were enrolled in the Division of Basic Studies. They remained in this division for advisement until they completed 60 semester hours. Changes dictated that if a second semester freshman declared a major in education and registered for the course, "Introduction to Teaching," a temporary advisor in education also had to be assigned to the student. These two advisors (experts in their own areas) were expected to collaborate on advisement and an appropriate program for the student. (Note: Due to the success of this procedure, the entire University adopted the plan to transfer potential majors to their intended College after completion of 23 prescribed hours.)

3. <u>Increasing the monitoring of student progress</u>. Explained in detail in Chapter 7.

4. <u>Keeping more complete records on students</u>. Historically, each advisor kept a curriculum sheet showing grades for completed courses and transcripts. Contemporary records also include: admission forms to the college, to the degree granting department, and to advanced level courses; college and departmental test data; and applications for admission to student teaching. It was envisioned that, from these records, an advisor could quickly retrieve students' demographic data, standardized test scores (including scores from NTE components), reading levels, grades, remediation experiences, and number of completed hours in early observation and participation teaching experiences.

5. <u>Providing more support to advisors and students through a new Office of Student Development and Academic Services</u>. This office was developed to assist advisors by (a) directing students desirous of majoring in education to appropriate departments, (b) providing initial advisement services to new students, (c) helping advisors to secure student records, (d) validating the work of advisors, (e) coordinating informational services to advisors and students, and (f) guiding faculty toward solution to advisement problems.

6. <u>Putting student data on computer</u>. Such technological support, it was believed, would make it possible for faculty to access student information more quickly, as well as allow them to conduct comparative studies of student performance. In addition, required reports would be easier to make.

Many positive rewards toward achieving excellence in teacher education occurred from these changes. Chief among them, however, was that the attitudes of students toward advisors, and vice versa, improved; student-faculty dialogue and interaction increased and more faculty members began making themselves available beyond regular office hours to advise students. Refinement of the system continues.

PREPARING EXTERNAL ENVIRONMENTS

Preparing environments external to the College of Education required building special give-and-take relationships. This is more a deduction from reviewing documentation and logic than a stated need. That a plan of action existed for this component also would be purely inference; a plan was never made public. College administrators seemed to approach the task, however, in a systematic and consistent manner.

Analysis of college records revealed that high on a probable administrative agendum was an objective to build attitudes of acceptance for Grambling among significant others across the nation. An apparent desire was to influence outsiders to (a) share expertise with Grambling's faculty, (b) provide information to help the College of Education anticipate problems and trends, (c) connect the college with potential funding sources, (d) serve as a national sounding board for Grambling's ideas, and (e) act in the future as conduits of information designed to dissipate Grambling's negative image among diverse academic audiences. Eventually, it was these external environments that first heralded Grambling's achievement.

By delineating indicators of the administration's need to prepare external environments for Grambling's change efforts, the task of describing how this need was addressed also can be accomplished. The indicators included the following:

- Having representatives, often the dean himself, to attend or participate in as many state, regional, and national conferences and meetings as possible.

- Searching out projects with similar objectives and establishing collaborative relationships.

- Volunteering faculty members to participate in state-sponsored activities such as validation of the new NTE, research on teacher assessment, and basic-skills competency testing for public schools.

- Having faculty members participate in validation activities for the new NTE sponsored by Educational Testing Service (ETS).

- Sending faculty consultants to other institutions and state agencies requesting services on test-wiseness for the NTE.

- Developing a College of Education newsletter as a forum for sharing information about the college and its progress.

- Consenting to interviews for newspaper articles about the college's improvement program.

- Applying for grants no matter how small and no matter the area as long as they were related to education.

- Participating in research activities conducted by other institutions.

- Bringing national leaders and experts to campus for sessions with faculty and students.

Whether planned or not, these activities did as much for Grambling's success as others. Many people would probably see such activities as unnecessary drains on an already taxed budget, but Grambling saw them as the basic necessities they turned out to be and funded them.

ORGANIZING HUMAN RESOURCES

The organization of human resources for change represented Grambling's desire for internal coherence in goal oriented work. Maximum productivity in a timely fashion was the goal. Toward this goal, college administrators began organizational maneuvers early in 1980. Faculty members demonstrating certain talents were matched to corresponding tasks. Similarly, people who had certain historical information were assigned to work with new persons who needed the information to complete their tasks. Depending on the day-to-day problems confronting the college, however, these functions and positions shifted.

Among the existing human resources within the college were several writers, a program developer, several curriculum specialists, many historians and critics, a documenter-evaluator, two strategists and human relations experts, and several self-trained academic politicians. To the college's disadvantage, though, several multi-talented people wore more than one of these hats. People with limited specialities stood by, unable to help or lamenting the burdens of their own workloads. Still others just stood by. This obvious waste of personnel was a perennial problem not unusual in academic organizations and not easy to overcome. At best, Grambling can claim only to have minimized this type of inaction, not to have eradicated it.

Besides organizing the work of individuals, the work of small faculty groups and administrators also was structured to serve the college in a number of ways. Functioning primarily as advisory bodies to the dean, the groups made recommendations for new policies and procedures, curriculum revision, solutions to emergent problems and needs, and new personnel. These same groups often wrote proposals, evaluated progress, undertook special research projects, conducted staff development sessions, and prepared pertinent reports. Included among the various college-level groups were:

> College of Education Council
>
> NTE Steering Committee
>
> Curriculum Revision Committee
>
> Recruitment Committee
>
> Committee for Apportionment of NTE Competencies
>
> Graduate Follow-up Study Committee
>
> Faculty Development Committee
>
> College of Education Proposal Development Team
>
> Advanced Seminar Teaching Team
>
> Education Resource Center Committee

Individual and group assignments usually originated with the dean. Once assignments were made, faculty members were free to suggest to the dean courses of action and ideas about handling a group's task. Many such suggestions were approved and implemented.

Organizing human resources for optimum productivity also meant structuring the ongoing business of the college so that, when necessary, workers were free of crippling interference. What could be the nature of such interference and of efforts to thwart it? An interview with the dean provides insightful clues.

According to the dean, experience indicated that in any change environment there are several types of people: drivers of moving vehicles (the innovators and workers), traffic cops (the traditionalists who, whether consciously or unconsciously, work to stop change), and the stalled vehicle operators (those nonworkers who straddle the fence between change and tradition). If change is going to take place as planned, traffic must be kept moving. This is an instance where even traffic cops can be in the way–interfering with the flow of traffic. Nonetheless, the dean suggested, provisions must be made to help these people maintain the integrity of their jobs. Even with their "blocking-type" behavior, they can be valuable, useful members to an organization. The important thing is, if these blockers serve the organization and if they are, at the same time, helped to stay out of the way of progress, they too can grow.

The approach taken by the dean in this case was the same as that used to achieve internal coherence in general: early in the process, matching people with tasks. A key difference, however, was that the traffic cops (i.e., blockers) were not assigned leadership roles for tasks deemed essential to the advancement of change, regardless of their expertise. They were instead leaders for maintenance and support-type activities. Additionally, the work of traffic cops and the consequences of their work were carefully monitored. Where it was possible to predict impending sabotage, measures were taken to deny them immediate access to project information and personnel. Increased maintenance workloads and travel to represent the college were two such measures.

Of significance here is not that the college faced a unique problem or even that it took innovative action to resolve the problem. The point is that the college anticipated a traffic-cop problem and planned for it early as part of its reorganization of human resources for change.

CONSULTANT'S NOTE #3:
GETTING A HANDLE
ON PROBLEMS AND PLANNING

The familiar adage, "Gather ye rosebuds while ye may," comes to mind. We had gathered all the problems. We knew a multitude of problems existed for the COE at all levels of the organization and all areas of teacher education. Thus interventions were going to be necessary inside and outside the College. We knew that the sources of pressures to improve student performance were many and diverse. Likewise, we knew there were internal forces acting upon the organization. People perceived themselves to be working hard, but getting nowhere. Their failure to get results led to a lack of job satisfaction, and for some, there seemed an overpowering desire to leave. Over time, others had adopted a lot of excuse-making and defeatist-type behavior. These people even questioned whether outsiders had the right to tell them (a) that Grambling's students had to pass the NTE, (b) what to teach in their courses, (c) who to admit to teacher education, and (d) when to graduate students. We were confronted with understanding the problems and planning a strategy for dealing with them.

An open-systems planning model was used for the examination. This model looks at inputs, throughputs (transformations), and outputs within an environment of forces acting upon the organization. The strategy was first to examine the future state, then to examine the present state, and finally to plan the transition state to be used.

To look at the faculty's and administration's visions of the future, COE departments were asked to generate objectives for three years. NTE performance was a primary target for measuring outcomes. The reason we started with this future state, or trying to determine what they wanted their future state to be like, was to avoid the demoralizing effects of playing "ain't it awful" and wallowing in the problems of the present state of performance on the NTE. My role as the consultant-trainer was to help the college look at a plan for its future through the goal-setting process.

Setting realistic goals and objectives in terms of identifiable outcomes is not always an easy task for academic units. Internal polarization, issues of territoriality, and personal ambition (or the lack thereof) often gets in the way. Experience suggests that it is much easier, given these conditions, for organizations to establish broad indefinite goals that allow for operating by seat-of-the-pants action. This approach, unfortunately, helps only to maintain the status quo and to keep an organization's level of anxiety, including creative anxiety, to a minimum.

As a victim of this predicament, Grambling's COE was confronted with the challenge to (a) develop a need for modifying its goal-setting process, (b) acquire more effective goal-setting and long-range planning skills, and (c) think about and set more realistic goals for itself.

Several training sessions were conducted in this area. I began the first session by asking the question: What are the things you can do without anyone else to begin to move toward the goals you've set for yourself? Together we reviewed available needs assessment data from varied perspectives: what they meant for the university, the college, and each department for certain, but also from the perspective of what they meant for individuals. Taking the organization methodically through these activities served both training and planning purposes. It increased the faculty's goal-setting skills while furthering development of their planned-change strategy. In assisting with this task, I found not too unusual results. The objectives initially were far too ambitious and needed to be modified. For example, the faculty wanted to move from a 6% to an 80% pass rate on the NTE in a year. Yet, it was evident that the people knew what they wanted to achieve. The fact that they had vision and wanted to get out there was encouraging, although they wanted to move faster than it looked possible. Part of my role at this time was saying, "Hey wait a minute. You want to make sure you succeed because success will give you energy. You don't want to fail this first year. Let's be realistic." Subsequent assistance from me in examining each objective by identifying forces for and against its accomplishment produced more realistic aspirations.

With outputs–the goals–tentatively established, at least for NTE performance, we looked at the present organization and system of teacher education and uncovered a multitude of attitudes and problems. These seemed to have been at all levels and at many points in the processes, the strategies, and the structures. It was apparent that interventions were needed inside and outside the college, that some of those outside forces were going to have to be changed–in general education for example. Some of the major areas in which people found problems are the following:

- Recruitment
- Admissions
- Orientation or socialization of students during their entry
- Advisement
- Curriculum
- Quality of instruction
- Staff development
- Screening for student teaching

- Screening for graduation

When we looked at the forces that were acting upon or sending the organization messages, we found these: the legislature, alumni, the State Department of Education, Higher Education Board, other schools and colleges within the university, and professional organizations and accrediting agencies (National Council for Accreditation for Teacher Education, American Association of Colleges for Teacher Education, Southern Association of Colleges and Schools). Also, the university's central administration itself was sending messages to the COE. There are at least four possible responses an organization can make to messages being sent to it by those forces making demands on the organization: ignore the message, kill or fight it, accept it and use it or change it.

Many messages were decoded by the leadership and response-choices were made. One of the overpowering problems, however, was the internal forces acting upon the organization. Because of what they read in the newspapers, what outsiders were saying about the COE, and what was being said to them in messages sent by such forces as the legislature, people in the COE felt bad about themselves. This was a dilemma for the COE. People wanted to feel good about themselves, but the results of their efforts were not promising enough to grant them this desire.

I saw this predicament as a symptom of failing organizational health. My approach was to begin with management to identifying the criteria for measuring the COE's organizational health and effectiveness. Beckhard's (1967) criteria were used as a guide. Central to the strategy were these factors:

1. Managing against well-defined goals and objectives

2. Allowing form to follow function

3. Providing for open communication

4. Matching rewards to work

5. Getting structural support for goals

6. Treating conflict as a problem to be managed

7. Minimizing unhealthy competition

8. Valuing the personal worth and dignity of individuals

Evidence showed that management, the dean and central administration, internalized these indicators of effectiveness quickly. For example, they had an early desire to reorganize the COE. After we examined the idea, the dean and central administration delayed that effort until they could look at some other things. In the process of talking about the idea, we discussed the fact that when managers move boxes around, they threaten a lot of people who are in the boxes. In consequence, much energy gets diverted to breaking out of boxes, rather than concentrated on desired outcomes. The dean decided not to restaff and reorganize immediately; he waited for functions to be more clearly defined. This was a demonstration of having understood, in particular, that form follows function. By and large this action signaled to me that the door to change and reform had been opened a little wider. Given this progress, planning for problem solving continued.

CHAPTER 4

OVERTURE FOR EXCELLENCE: TOWARD A PROGRAM PLAN

That the College of Education had a program improvement plan up to this point is not really true. What it had was a procedure for arriving at a plan. This procedure was based upon a well defined philosophical base among whose anchors are three critical beliefs stressed throughout this document. Because of their importance to planning and to the entire success story, these beliefs are listed below:

1. Paramount to test scores, a quality teacher preparation program, in general, must be developed and installed.

2. Testing is a reality. Educators can get no where by fighting tests. Their energies must be directed toward mastering them.

3. The student performance problem, on tests and otherwise, belongs to the university—not just to the College of Education; so, the University must be influenced to share in the problem's solution. Nevertheless, since the College of Education stands to lose the most and to lose it first, the college must change, beginning with its own programmatic contributions.

Under this orientation, the college sought in 1980 to move from a set of goals and no program plan to several miniprogram plans. Why miniprogram plans? The college's continually evolving data base surfaced six major themes or areas for improvement: immediate improvement in the NTE pass rate, student assessment, faculty development, curriculum revision, instructional development, and program monitoring and evaluation. Because these areas appeared to require massive adjustments, separate improvement plans for each area were presumed advantageous. First, smaller modules of work possibly would keep faculty from becoming overwhelmed and immobilized by the gigantic picture. Short-term successes would be more frequent and visible and would enkindle motivation intermittently. Second, miniplans would allow the college to stagger development of program components on the basis of available human and material resources; inability to move in one area would not necessarily affect program improvement in another. Third, pinpointing effective and ineffective activities in the change process would be made easier. Fourth, miniplans would simplify isolating certain programs for presentation to potential external funding sources. Fifth, this approach was likely to give the college more than one source of power, that is, the college would have several entry points toward goal achievement.

Although the planning process was decentralized, there lurked the desire for separate yet interrelated, independent but interdependent plans that together would represent a macroprogram strategy. The conceptual glue, in this case, was mutual expectations for common outcomes toward achievement of a common goal.

A PLAN EMERGES

Planning did not turn out as decentralized as designed. Proposal developers over-planned. The proposal's title, A National Teacher Examinations Improvement Program, was correct, but the suggested program was a comprehensive strategy providing for all the major areas of need uncovered by the college's research findings. Eventually this heuristic product (the proposed program) became the forerunner to Grambling's present day program model.

The original NTE improvement proposal included the following objectives:

1. To develop and implement a teacher training program that reflects consideration for the sixteen competency areas measured by the NTE.

2. To develop and implement teacher training requirements that facilitate the acquisition of appropriate teaching behavior skills by preservice teachers in the areas of classroom management, schools as organizations, and interpersonal skills for teachers.

3. To develop and implement a strategy that provides a diagnostic/prescriptive approach to remediating all deficiencies that might affect the students' classroom and competency-testing performance.

4. To supplement training in the fundamental skill areas of reading and problem solving (cognitive processing).

5. To provide faculty in the College of Education a support system that facilitates and enhances classroom instruction.

6. To develop and implement a process of staff development that organizes and synchronizes the instructional efforts of all faculty toward improving NTE scores.

The program was designed to reach full maturity by fall 1982, after commencing in spring 1981. With full implementation, appreciable differences in students' NTE scores were projected to appear in the February 1982 test results, if not sooner. On reflection, this was indeed an ambitious schedule for such a complex design.

Summary of Program Components

Figure 1 summarizes the originally proposed program components in flowchart format. Descriptions of each component follow in the next section.

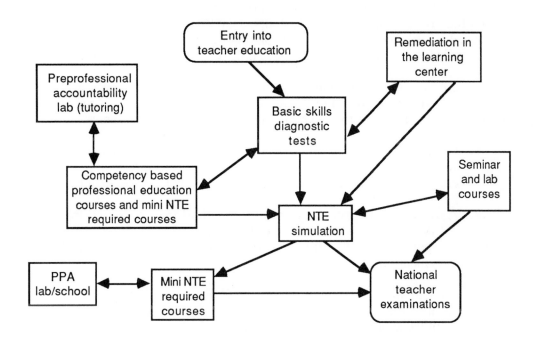

Figure 1

Grambling's Initial Program Improvement Strategy

The Basic Skills Diagnostic Program

Grambling's students have always had to complete 60 hours in general studies including basic skills subjects, and additional hours in remedial/developmental work, if necessary, before entering the teacher education program. Moreover, the University has operated a developmental education program to remediate student deficiencies in basic skills. The performance of many students exiting general studies in the early 80's indicated a need for further remediation in reading and communication skills. The deficiencies students brought to the College of Education from those colleges offering the general education components of the overall teacher education program and the inability of the education faculty to be all things to all students, contributed greatly to students' poor performance on the NTE and in professional education courses. Consideration of these factors led to the proposal for a basic skills diagnostic program component.

To correct student deficiencies and at the same time to help reclaim and reestablish the true mission of the teacher education program, it was proposed that the following steps be taken toward realizing the diagnostic component.

1. Competency requirements in the areas of reading and oral and written communication should be spelled out and established as entry criteria for all students seeking to pursue teaching majors.

2. Assessment instruments should be identified or developed to measure the extent to which applicants attained required competencies in the stipulated areas before admission to the College of Education.

3. Student applicants for entry into the College of Education should be administered the above-mentioned instruments and required to make a critical score for acceptance into a specific teaching program.

4. Student applicants not making required scores should be conditionally admitted and allowed to pursue teacher education courses for a specified period on a contractual basis. Conditional admission requirements included the following:

   a. Students must attend the University Learning Center (subsequently renamed the Academic Skills Center) for remedial instruction in deficit areas and maintain a log of activities and progress validated by center personnel. Students also had the alternative to pursue self-initiated study to alleviate their deficiencies.

b. At the end of the two semesters, following remedial instruction, students must take an interim basic skills test that indicates academic progress.

c. At the end of the two regular semesters and one summer session, conditional majors will be terminated if they fail to achieve critical scores in the basic skills areas as required by the college. Terminated majors may seek re-entry after meeting entry standards if they have no grades of less than *B* in professional education courses taken as conditional students.

Installation of any new program demands that special consideration be given to students already matriculating under previously established program guidelines. Installation of the basic skills diagnostic component was no exception. Provisions were made for students admitted to the teacher education program under old guidelines: (a) students in this category who had a year or less left on a plan of study would be given an opportunity to complete their training regardless of their diagnostic test scores. (b) newly developed basic skills competencies would become exit criteria for incoming students and students who had more than a year of work to complete on existing plans of study.

5. Existing students in the College of Education should take a battery of diagnostic and competency tests immediately after they were identified so that corrective work can begin and delays in graduation can be avoided.

6. The College of Education should ensure that existing students were not unduly penalized by new program requirements. These requirements should be made available to advanced students and incoming freshmen who might be affected by them as soon as possible. Also, advisors, faculty members in the College of Education, Basic Studies, Liberal Arts and Science and Technology, as well as administrators, should be notified and provided with the information necessary for preparing students for careers in education.

Implicit in the six steps was that the Diagnostic Unit would act as a pivot for feeding information into the teacher preparation system at several points. Figure 2, shows the unit's linking characteristics.

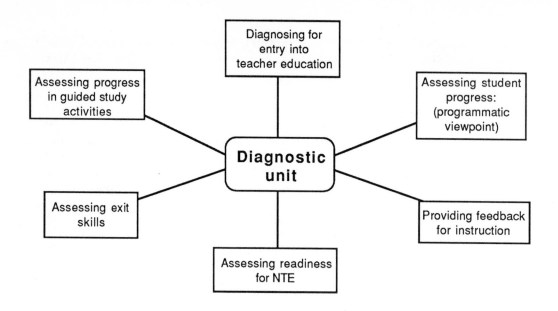

Figure 2

Linkages of The Diagnostic Unit

In sum, the proposed diagnostic component was expected to provide for a teacher preparation program firmly grounded in diagnostic/prescriptive training. It was envisioned as flexible and capable of adjusting to changes in students, faculty members, the profession, and society.

Competency-Based Professional Education Course Design

The course design component was intended to have the most immediate impact on teacher education majors, their instructors, and professional education courses offered by the College of Education. This component proposed the reorganization and enhancement of the professional training curriculum toward increased responsiveness to testing and the basic skills needs of students.

Essentially, competency-based course designs meant that, consistent with the 16 NTE competency areas, student performance objectives would be apportioned to and covered in appropriate professional education courses. Each affected course would be redesigned to include a NTE type mini-test focusing specifically on the content to be taught in that course. It was proposed that students be required to demonstrate mastery of test items at the 90 percent level. Further, where such mastery was not attained, it was proposed that students receive remediation in the Preprofessional Accountability Laboratory, the third program component.

Preprofessional Accountability Laboratory

The Preprofessional Accountability Laboratory was intended as a support system for all education faculty members and students, but especially for those connected with proposed competency-based courses. Remediation in the basic skills and professional education was envisioned as the laboratory's primary function. Second and third functions included providing selected students with practical experiences in test taking, and performing diagnostic services for students attempting entry into the college or a teaching program.

Ideally the Preprofessional Accountability Laboratory was expected to (a) provide students an atmosphere conducive for studying and seeking academic tutoring or other assistance, (b) enhance student motivation for learning, (c) improve the study habits of students by providing them practice and training in appropriate study (how to study) behavior, (d) facilitate diagnostic/prescriptive teacher training, and (e) implement monitoring and support systems for the independent study assignments made by faculty members. The laboratory program, if properly executed, promised to increase the instructional range of faculty members without unduly burdening them with additional work. It also promised to increase the faculty's capacity for individualizing instruction. Three clusters of student-centered activities were identified to operationalize the aspect of the laboratory component.

1. **Student Initiated Study (SIS) Unit.** This unit was to provide students opportunities to attend the Laboratory voluntarily to study professional education materials. Except for those materials placed in a "Restricted Use Area" by faculty members, all laboratory materials were to be made available to students. By keeping a student roster or record of laboratory attendance, data automatically would be available for monitoring, assessment, and research purposes.

2. **Guided Independent Study (GIS) Unit.** This unit was designed to operate on a contract system between instructors and students. Contracts were to involve whatever activities the laboratory sponsored or arranged. Activities prepared by faculty or purchased by laboratory personnel also were considered appropriate resources. Since laboratory personnel would be monitoring and validating the completion of contracts, it was

suggested that faculty agree upon and design contract forms and processes.

3. **Individual Student Instruction (ISI) Unit.** Expectations were that many students who visited the laboratory would not know how to (a) use laboratory services, (b) study topics across a number of references and sources, (c) interpret certain professional terms, (d) infer from information, (e) initiate problem solving, and (f) interpret an assignment. This tutorial unit was designed to provide individual students with such training.

FACING THE PLAN:
APPREHENSION, PROCRASTINATION, FRUSTRATION

Accomplishment of several prerequisite tasks seemed in order for a project of the magnitude and importance of the improvement proposal. These tasks were to (a) assess human resources and physical plant facilities, (b) become familiar with existing program structures and operations, and (c) determine the priorities of people who would be involved and who would implement the program if approved.

Upon closer scrutiny, a college committee ascertained that only portions of the program improvement NTE proposal could be implemented immediately; that these activities must be initiated concurrently with other project long-term undertakings; and that the proposed program must be refined as conditions dictated. With these caveats and some minor modifications, this threshold program received approval from the college near the end of 1981. Implementation and program modifications transpired over a second year under the management of the college's NTE Steering Committee.

Proposal developers, college administrators, and the NTE Steering Committee thought that approval of the teacher education improvement proposal signaled readiness for implementation. They were wrong. Instead, approval instigated questions from faculty members that had remained dormant for months. Some of their questions were manifestations of apprehension, procrastination, and frustration. Of the answers that were given or could be given at this time, however, most helped to crystallize in everyone's minds the relationship between the program goal and program philosophy; between paper ideas and expectations for action, and between college of education faculty members and faculties across campus. Two of the most significant questions and answers follow.

First, where should change begin? Proposal developers indicated that the suggested program was designed to originate at the departmental level. Given the nature of the target student population, it seemed not only fitting that the Department of Teacher Education be a starting point, but also logical that this department should be a main source of leadership for others, internal and external to the college.

Concerns shared in support of a departmental approach were expressed by the education faculty during a staff development session in 1980 and by faculty members across campus given in response to a survey also conducted in 1980. Some of these concerns appear below.

The place where the process of improving NTE scores should begin is in the various departments. There should be an effort made by the College of Education to coordinate its attack on low NTE scores with faculty in departments outside the college. Currently, there is no concerted effort being made in any such department–at least, not to my knowledge

*****

Teacher education majors seldom come to avail themselves of our services because we are not in the College of Education.

*****

There needs to be an effective advisement program (for the NTE) at all classification levels in each department serving education majors.

*****

There should be general and area tests in each department. Majors should be given a list of the information they need to know (or read) to pass the test. This list should be provided as soon as students transfer to education from general studies.

*****

Second, how available would support services be to faculty and students for making NTE improvements? Interestingly, faculty members outside the college felt that existing services were adequate, while most faculty members in the College of Education believed just the opposite. According to the ad hoc NTE committee charged with searching for an answer to this question, all faculty members tended generally to agree that teacher education majors seldom used the services of the University Learning Center, the University Curriculum Resource Center, or the Social Science Skills Center. In reviewing the definitions and offerings of these various resource units, the committee discovered that, except for the Social Science Skills Center, all available services specified freshmen as the target population. In effect, there were few services at the university for students at the sophomore level and above.

A three-hour visit to Grambling Hall to review the remedial and developmental academic units that comprised the University Learning Center supported this finding. Interviews with various center personnel revealed the following:

- Although services were available to all students, the center was generally prepared to serve freshmen and a few sophomores.

- Only one advanced-level education major was receiving remedial instruction on a regular basis; this student was the exception because of a unique and acute problem.

- Few media materials were available for teaching majors in the professional education area. An increase in these offerings was doubtful because of funding priorities for the center.

- Even if materials were available and more students did seek assistance at the center, insufficient personnel were available to serve them.

- The stability of certain services in the center were suspect because their operations and survival depended upon funding from grants.

In its report, the ad hoc NTE committee made the following additional recommendations to the college:

1. That existing required professional education courses be reviewed to ascertain the extent to which additional objectives related to NTE competencies should be added to course content. (This was consistent with proposed competency-based course designs.)

64

2. That the College of Education work with the University Learning Center to provide prospective education majors improved learning resources in the basic skills and professional education areas.

3. That the College of Education encourage students not to take the NTE until they received some form of instruction in test taking; further, that the college provide this instruction beyond what was being given. Specifically, education majors should be advised to take the actual NTE for a first time no earlier than November of their senior year; and, such advisement should depend upon previous student performance on NTE minitests, NTE simulation scores, and student progress after the simulation.

4. That the Preprofessional Accountability Laboratory be given top priority for development with immediate attention to its capacity for diagnosing and assessing students' competencies. Further, the laboratory should also assume responsibility for administering and reporting the results of all tests: diagnostic NTE minitests, NTE simulations, and other examinations for which faculty members contracted.

5. That a full-time faculty position be funded to manage and operate the Preprofessional Accountability Laboratory, and that the person hired in this new position be trained in testing and remediating students.

Other questions raised by faculty members and students at this stage also were important. Will faculty get release time to develop or revise courses? How can the college get more students to take the test-awareness course and attend the coaching seminars? Who will be responsible for monitoring student progress? Where will the money come from for additional remediation materials? What generic teaching skills do we want students to have regardless of whether these skills are required on the NTE? When faculty identify students who need remediation, who will see that they get it? Will the additional demands made of students by the college cause them to suffer academic overload? Will the demands cause students to select majors other than teaching?

At the outset, the college was without answers to these questions, but it documented each of them. In later years the college offered answers, revised its initial answers, and, in some instances, revised its revisions–all in search of those sometimes elusive correct responses.

CHAPTER 5

NO U-TURNS:
COMPREHENSIVE CURRICULUM REVISION

The college had in place a series of courses prescribed for each of the teacher education program majors: early childhood, elementary, secondary, special, and all-levels education. What it did not have in place was a clearly described curriculum amenable to concrete terms; a description of the knowledge, skills, attitudes, and behaviors that program graduates were expected to possess upon exit; or a clearly articulated and well-understood linkage between the graduate's program of study and skills and competencies. Simply stated, the college had a teacher training curriculum that could be contributing to the problem of poor student performance on the NTE rather than solving it. No one seemed sure.

The College of Education found itself in a period of instability, a highly volatile situation for programs, faculty, students, and administrators. Bombarded with the existing data base and determined to avoid the "ostrich syndrome," administrators and faculty raised serious curricular questions for the system of teacher education. What should be the objectives of the teaching programs? What should the preservice teacher be like on completing the program at Grambling State University? What should students learn? How could the College of Education provide leadership in reconciling varying philosophical persuasions and blending them into a unified whole? How could the college balance the influence of societal pressures, student needs, and approved professional practice? What should the college be doing for its own preservice teachers and for promoting improvement in the educational systems throughout the state and nation? What was the existing curriculum like? What were its strengths and its faults? (This question highlighted the need for curriculum analysis.) What, in fact, was the existing curriculum? What did it purport to do? What did it actually do? Where were the gaps? Where were the overlaps?

GOALS OF CURRICULUM ANALYSIS AND REVISION

Answering these and similar questions became a goal of curriculum analysis activities. A second desired outcome of curriculum analysis and subsequent revision efforts was to increase faculty accountability for the curriculum. As with many other programs, the curriculum in teacher education had been developed around a conceptual framework, but responses to legislative mandates, developments in education in general and teacher education in specific, revised certification requirements, and changes in the professional directions of learned societies had resulted in a curriculum quite different from its origin. The curriculum had become dated, planned at a time when expectations were less stringent and planned for a clientele with a different set of characteristics.

These changes, in conjunction with new faculty on staff who had little orientation to the original framework, seemed to have resulted in fragmented views of what the program was intended to do, of what the graduate should be like and of what contribution each course should make in student development. Faculty members seemed to view the curriculum as a series of courses, not a whole program. In turn, this fragmented view resulted in lack of a clear relationship among the content being taught, instructional methodology being employed in any given course, and expected performances of students completing the program. It became difficult for professors to visualize that what they did or did not do in a given course actually made (or should have made) an impact on the teaching performance and NTE test scores of program graduates. The dimmer the vision of that relationship became, the less accountable individual professors seemed to feel for success. Likewise, the relationship between input and program output in terms of student products became vaguer. In addition, the links between the teaching activities of professors and their feelings of responsibility to and for teaching majors became weaker.

Increased awareness and acknowledgment of the cause-effect relationship among course objectives, instructional methodology, and student success on competence measures and classroom performance was necessary. Since in its broadest definition *curriculum* is the sum of all learning experiences under the auspices of the organizational unit, the cause-effect relationship had also to be established for student experiences other than education courses. Advisement, student organizations sponsored by the COE, tutorial activities, and COE-sponsored professional development activities for students and faculty had to be considered.

Establishing faculty accountability became a high-priority goal of the curriculum analysis and revision process. Administrators and planners were keenly aware that even the most innovative, educationally sound, and well-conceived curriculum could not solve the problems confronting the college without the key element of faculty accountability.

The third goal of the analysis and review process was increased teacher effectiveness in facilitating student achievement of curriculum goals and objectives specifically identified for courses each professor taught. Although most of the courses taught by COE professors had rigor, students were not always held accountable for attainment of a specific set of skills and objectives as long as the student performed satisfactorily overall. That is, students could excel in one part of a course and fail miserably in another part, but still squeak by when their performances were averaged. The intent of curriculum analysis and revision was to assist faculty in targeting sets of skills and competencies that a student must demonstrate before exiting the course. With this intent, curriculum revision also aimed to promote student accountability for development and demonstration of specified competencies.

The fourth objective for curriculum analysis and revision was to update curriculum content in response to contemporary issues such as increased infusion of the research base on teaching into the preparation program. In conjunction with this phase, measures were undertaken to use the knowledge base for professional education as a tool to guide other curricular decisions.

ANALYSIS AND REVISION PROCESS

Existing data questioned the effectiveness of the present curriculum in preparing students for success, particularly on such measures as the NTE. Curriculum analysis and revision was vital. But how should the COE undertake the process in the most expeditious, yet effective, manner? Again, program planners in the COE were "plowing new ground," because there was no model, no tried and proven technique to guide the process. Brainstorm sessions yielded no great approach, only a common-sense direction for the process.

Curriculum Analysis. The first phase involved an analysis of the existing curriculum in teacher education with respect to current research, sociopolitical pressures, approved professional practices, and faculty values. For two years beforehand, faculty and administrators in the COE had been engaged in identifying competencies that were deemed essential for all program graduates. This activity resulted in a list of essential competencies, the generic teaching competencies and faculty agreed that all professional courses should seek to promote these. The competencies became one of three focal points for review and analysis of existing curriculum content. A second focal point was the existing scientific basis for teaching, including the body of research on teaching that had emerged in recent years. A third focal point was the set of competencies identified by the Educational Testing Service for successful performance on the core battery of the NTE. By putting together these three ingredients, the planners responded to the research in the field, the desires and values of the faculty, and the sociopolitical forces of preparing students for success on standardized competence measures. These three sets of data became the standards by which the curriculum would be analyzed to test the degree of congruence between what was required in the curriculum to produce the expected competent graduate and what was already present in the curriculum.

To test for congruence, the existing curriculum, identified as its component courses, was charted and presented for review. The faculty in the COE reviewed the professional education curriculum, while general education and portions of the specialized academic curriculum underwent a separate review.

In the professional education curriculum review, the faculty identified the appropriate course in which each item on all three lists was currently being developed. The analytical test revealed what several professors and administrators already suspected: (1) some competencies were being targeted in most courses; (2) some competencies were being addressed in none; (3) some competencies were introduced in one or more courses, but mastery was demanded in none; (4) some courses assumed little or none of the burden for contributing to the competence of the program graduate, while few courses assumed much of the burden; (5) professors tended to assume that even though specific competencies were not targeted in the course they taught, the competencies were being addressed in those courses taught by one or more of their colleagues; and (6) the faculty placed a disproportionate number of competencies for mastery as an expectation for the advanced methods courses (one each for elementary, early childhood, and secondary-level majors).

The general education component and the specialized academic component of the curriculum external to the COE also underwent analysis under the same criteria as the professional education component. The college took a leadership role in stimulating this effort. This process consisted of the making respective department heads and faculty aware of the competency demands specific to their content area; meeting with the respective administrators and faculty to share student performance data; requesting in-depth matching of required competencies and required courses; requesting specific courses and other student experience recommendations that would satisfy the identified competencies; requesting course revisions to provide a greater degree of congruence between course objectives, activities and competence expectations; and requesting development where no courses existed to satisfy student competence needs in those respective areas.

Other finite curriculum analyses became a function of the specific department from which required courses were taught. For example, following requests from the COE, the department head and faculty in mathematics examined the required curriculum in that area as it related to competencies required for success on standardized measures such as the NTE. Not unlike what the College of Education curriculum analysis revealed, these general education curriculum audits also revealed serious gaps as well as some overlapping. Results of the analyses of all components of the curriculum supported further reform. There were glaring discrepancies centering upon the nature of the curriculum, what it prepared learners to do, and what it used as performance measures for success.

Apportionment of Competencies. The curriculum audit revealed the gaps to be streamlined. Now that the Steering Committee knew what needed to happen to the curriculum, the problem became deciding *how* to make it happen quickly and effectively. Committee members decided to involve faculty as much as possible in the process.

Results of faculty assessments and assignments of course-specific competencies surfaced a noteworthy observation. It seemed that as they were stated, the NTE competencies could reasonably be developed in any, and all, of the courses assigned by the faculty. The committee members feared that such an arrangement would certainly elude any form of accountability, a goal of the process. The fear was that individual faculty members would assume that other courses and other faculty members were addressing the NTE competencies, so everyone would think the problem would be solved but nothing would actually be done. At this point questions emerged. Could the efforts bear fruit with such nebulous responsibilities, or would a more finite description be necessitated? Should the charted curriculum with attendant responsibilities go back for more intensive faculty scrutiny? Given the fatigue of the faculty with the task, would another in-depth review even be beneficial? Given the matchings recommended by the faculty for courses, could individual interpretations of the broadly stated competencies have been an intervening variable in the process?

With little else to go on except a hunch, the committee members recommended that further work on curriculum revision be halted until staff development sessions explicating the broad NTE competence list be implemented. Briefly, these sessions, described fully in Chapter 6, took the form of individual faculty study of sample tests from the ETS "dead file" and planned staff sessions with ETS officials. As short-term consultants, the persons presented item-by-item analyses of Grambling's student performance during recent NTE administrations.

When the faculty reconvened to compare the work done in staff development with prior COE efforts at assigning competency to specific courses, the faculty and committee concluded that much of what had been done was invalid. In fact, faculty interpretations of what the NTE competencies meant were far off the mark. What the faculty thought a competency meant was not necessarily what the NTE items measured. Nor was much of what was being taught consistent with the content suggested by the test items. As a result, the faculty no longer volunteered that a specific competency was introduced, reinforced, or mastered in their particular courses. Rather, they expressed surprise and frustration about what they had learned.

Assigned responsibility for facilitating the curriculum revision process in a timely manner, the committee members felt defeated when it became evident that the process was back at square one. Much time and effort had been expended, but still an overwhelming proportion of the task remained to be done. Expediency became the byword. Committee members decided that taking the task back in its present state to an obviously frustrated faculty would be tantamount to continued delays and diminished returns. Thus, the committee decided that the apportionment activities could be completed most expeditiously by a few people, namely, committee members.

The next steps consisted of listing all courses in sequence of pursuit, considering all competencies to be developed by students and reasoning a logical sequence for level of difficulty, matching competencies with courses, assessing the "goodness of fit," and adjusting all competencies and courses until the committee thought that the resulting scope and sequence chart was educationally sound and practically implementable. In short, this effort required (1) a task-analysis of the three component content foci: NTE specific competencies, generic teaching competencies, and research base on teaching; (2) sequencing of the component tasks into proficiency levels: introductory, reinforcement or maintenance, and mastery; and (3) deliberate, calculated, and systematic assignment of the component competencies to courses in the professional sequence. The decision to apportion competencies to courses in this prescriptive fashion was not taken lightly and it was not without anticipated consequences; particularly expected were charges of infringement on the professors' academic freedom. In fact, though, none of the negative responses occurred. When the decisions were shared with faculty, and implications for their accountability were discussed at a subsequent faculty meeting, only positive comments indicating acceptance of the apportionment report were heard. Such comments as these were made.

- "This is what we really needed to do. It will help us synchronize our efforts."

- "If this will allow us to help our students negotiate the NTE successfully, I'm all for it."

- "This seems a fair and equitable distribution of the workload and the responsibilities."

The apportionment charts, presented for review and reactions, were unanimously approved by COE faculty without alterations. Further, the faculty voted to initiate implementation efforts immediately. It seemed that Committee members and faculty alike believed that the apportionment effort held potential for success. In fact, the efforts resulted in a curriculum structure that was tighter than the structure used previously: a course assigned responsibility for each desired student competency; a sensible distribution of competencies across the curriculum from the advanced freshman to the senior year; more equitable distribution of competency-development expectations of courses across the curriculum; and a sense of accountability by professors to the curriculum, to the students, and to professional colleagues for promoting competency development. The drive to achieve excellence in the curriculum was officially underway.

Revision and Curriculum Implementation. The apportionment efforts highlighted the need for additional curriculum revision, particularly in redesigning some courses, deleting some, and adding others. This was the third phase in the curriculum revision process. Once competencies were apportioned,

COE professors began to design course syllabi according to a standardized format which specified generic competencies, the National Teacher Examination competencies and the level of expected course responsibility (i.e., to introduce, to reinforce, or to promote mastery of the competencies).

Because the COE also held ultimate responsibility for the total teacher education program and for the student performance although part of the program was taught through departments external to the College, the COE sought to maintain the right and responsibility to influence curriculum and instruction germane to teacher preparation regardless of the administrative unit. Leaning upon this fact, the COE realized that it would have to take action in the general education curriculum component. Scrutiny of this component also uncovered needs for curriculum revision, altering course requirements, altering course descriptions and components, and developing new courses. For example, the mathematics apportionment audit revealed that a large number of NTE competencies were being addressed by none of the mathematics courses required for teaching majors. The COE recommended two courses of action: that majors be required to take a different set of mathematics courses which did address the competencies, and that an existing mathematics course be altered sufficiently to include the competencies. The Mathematics Department complied.

The audit revealed a gap in competencies related to composition and modern literature. This information, when shared with the English Department, had similarly helpful results. To meet competency requirements, the English Department proposed: (1) a change in the sequence of English courses required for teaching majors; (2) development, implementation and requirement of a new course to promote mastery of competencies not addressed by existing courses; and (3) implementation of policy to increase the quantity and quality of students' writing products throughout existing English courses.

Similarly, the social science department made recommendations based upon the audits. These included changing the sequence of required courses, updating existing courses to reflect more nearly the demands made for successful performance on the NTE.

The professional education curriculum component called for other changes in addition to the apportionment of competencies. Professional courses were sequenced so that the component would reflect appropriate learner characteristics at each stage of professional development. The new and redesigned existing courses and professional experiences, along with their sequences are described as follows:

1. A second-semester, freshman-level course was developed and implemented. This course was designed to promote careful and systematic orientation of the interested student to teaching, to the teaching program and its requirements and expectations, and to

practical experiences in local schools. This new course was assigned specific competencies and was created to respond to other gaps evidenced in the curriculum review.

2. A sophomore-level, seminar-type course was created to provide introductory-level and some maintenance-level competency development. This course, too, responded to gaps revealed by the curriculum audits and apportionment activities.

3. Senior-level advanced methods courses were designed. These courses, traditionally one for each specific content major or area of certification, were collapsed into a single course to be pursued by all majors in common. This advanced methods course became a key point for (a) demonstration of mastery of the competencies on the extended competency list and (b) systematic infusion of the research base on teaching. Divided into two major components–generic teaching skills and specialized academic teaching skills–this seminar-type course responded to a wide array of student and program needs.

   • It had a heavy burden of competencies expected for mastery, both generic and NTE.

   • It filled gaps in both academic and professional development of students.

   • It provided experiences intended to influence both cognitive and affective dimensions of the emerging professional.

   • It dealt with the "wholeness" of the students, the full gamut of their development needs.

   • And in the words of a student in the course, the "seminar was not a course you take. It was an experience that you share."

4. A systematic, well-designed, and appropriately sequenced plan was developed for professional laboratory experiences. Administrators in the college recognized that curriculum was more than courses and plans of study. It also was comprised of the events one experienced, analyzed, and perceived as meaningful. Thus, curriculum revision efforts also focused upon planning for and arranging for professional laboratory experiences at all levels of the preparation program. The plan identified types of experiences; variety in school types, student clientele, environmental settings, etc.; and specified a minimum of required experiences for students at

73

each level of their professional development, culminating in a minimum requirement of 100 hours prior to student teaching.

5. A plan for systematic monitoring and inservice professional development for student teachers was devised. The course, "Student Teaching," was also apportioned a series of NTE and generic competencies for development, most at the mastery level. Special inservice workshops were installed to address competency development and to facilitate faculty and peer support and assistance as student teachers translated theory into classroom practice. These direct inservice training workshops averaged about 70 clock hours of instruction per semester.

OTHER CURRICULAR DECISIONS AND INNOVATIONS

Decisions based on curriculum analysis and subsequent actions taken resulted in a curriculum responsive to (a) social and political forces demanding a specific type of performance from students on competence measures, (b) the research base on teaching, and (c) faculty expectations for what the student should be like upon graduation. Although major efforts dealt with curriculum content, other areas of concern were not entirely omitted. The curriculum-analysis activities always were superimposed on the issues of characteristics of the learners, their previous achievement, interests, learning styles, cognitive levels, etc.; principles of learning; and general resources available. These concerns gave rise to a number of curriculum revisions that targeted specific needs of the current and intended clientele. The Steering Committee believed that these efforts would result in more responsive curricula and instruction, and in greater student learning.

Revision efforts promised major long-range benefits; but what about students already in the teaching programs who would not be exposed to this revised curriculum? What approach should be taken, or bandages applied, to address the academic needs of these students? The COE worked long and successfully with students who had real potential but evidenced a poor history of performance on standardized measures.

Responding to the needs of the learners already pursuing the program, curriculum revision efforts focused on designing experiences for students who, although completing required content courses prior to revisions, still showed deficits in expected content and process competencies. The COE expanded its role as faculty accepted a defined responsibility to address all student deficiencies. This manifested itself in at least two observable ways: incorporation of basic skills curriculum (particularly in the language skills areas) into existing courses, and development of basic skills courses. Initially, two three-semester hour accountability courses were developed for students needing remediation in reading and communication skills. The reading course focused on improvement of reading speed and reading comprehension, particularly at inferential and critical levels, while the course in English focused on listening comprehension and written comprehension. Both courses identified generic teaching and NTE competencies to be mastered by teaching majors. Although neither was required, students whose diagnostic profiles indicated weaknesses in various competence areas were encouraged by advisors and department heads to pursue the courses or other experiences that would alleviate observed weaknesses. Later, a third course for students with content and problem-solving weaknesses in mathematics was added. This course's format was similar to those in reading and communication skills.

Not only did the college respond to the needs of students with course additions, it also developed and installed a Basic Skills Diagnostic-Remediation Component. Described in detail earlier in this document, the diagnostic-remedial program provided student assessment services in the basic skills areas. It also provided opportunities for amelioration of student deficiencies, including the provision of a tutorial program, particularly for mathematics and English. Staffed by volunteer professors from the College of Education *and* other colleges throughout the university and graduate assistants, the tutorial program operated on a late afternoon and early evening basis to accommodate the schedules of students. Tutors used generic teaching and NTE competencies as the objectives for individual and small group tutorial sessions. Tutoring was tailored to the unique needs of each student, as defined by a student's diagnostic profile.

Because the college accepted the definition of curriculum as the total learning experiences, planned and unplanned, secured by students, planners were concerned with experiences of the learners beyond courses. Some of these experiences included:

- Provision of a microcomputer laboratory with software targeting a wide range of information including basic skills, general professional knowledge, and NTE specific competencies.

- Provision of an extensive list of curriculum materials for student exploration and use.

- Provision of an Media Production Laboratory with opportunities for preparing teacher-made learning aids, for learning to use a variety of instructional media equipment and materials.

- Provision of a simulated classroom with opportunities for students to (1) arrange physical classroom environments to meet a variety of instructional choices and decisions (2) engage in peer-teaching, (3) make video recordings of teaching episodes and analysis/critique of teaching performance, and (4) analyze actual curriculum materials in use in local K-12 school systems.

CONCLUDING PERSPECTIVES

The COE conducted curriculum analysis as a data source on which to plan future directions. At several points during the process of striving for excellence in teacher education, the college struggled for answers and agonized over decisions. During the curriculum analysis and decision phase, research data supported choices to respond to public pressures for improved student performance on the NTE by setting in motion a plan that would facilitate student success. The fact that the curriculum evidenced gaps in general education, professional education, and specialized academic components–that entire categories of competencies were not being addressed adequately by the existing curriculum–supported the notion that Grambling State University could improve the performance of its students on the NTE if the correct decisions were made and implemented at the appropriate time, before it was too late–for the student and the program.

What were the outcomes of curriculum reform? In large measure, the original goals and expected outcomes were realized. These included: (1) competency-based course designs; (2) a curriculum that developed sequentially and systematically students' competencies in generic teaching skills and NTE specific competence areas; (3) a curriculum with enhanced responsiveness to student needs, specifically in testing and basic skills areas; (4) a diagnostic/prescriptive component supporting student development of basic skills and other competencies; and (5) a general education component analyzed and redesigned by respective departments under the College of Education's leadership.

Less easily identifiable and quantifiable outcomes also were in evidence. Faculty members in the College of Education realized how much each component of the curriculum contributed to student development. They also realized how any competence that a student failed to develop in any given class could undermine his or her potential success on NTE. They began to expect each course to make its contribution, each professor to hold himself or herself, as well as the students, accountable for what happened in a course. This expectation extended to faculty and courses in the general education component as well.

Essentially, the faculty also began to accept responsibility for addressing basic skills development in all courses by adjusting requirements and standards for satisfactory performance, particularly in the area of communication skills. Increased involvement in and expectations for higher quality written assignments was a major new requirement for students across the curriculum.

Students also changed. As required competencies were explained to them, students began to realize that their education must be more than what they did in classes. Self-initiated study was a prerequisite for success rather than a spare-time amusement.

Interestingly, as the curriculum tightened and performance standards grew more stringent, an education major subculture began to emerge. Subculture characteristics were evident by the time students enrolled in "Seminar II: Advanced Methods" (usually during the first semester senior year) and were clearly developed by the time students were ready for student teaching. Among these characteristics were: (1) self-imposed, peer-enforced dress and conduct codes including class attendance, (2) highly developed peer-support groups for academic and personal growth, (3) an endearing sense of colleagueship among teaching majors, and (4) a willingness to inculturate new majors into the teacher education society.

Although the COE's steps were in imperceptibly small increments, other changes in the curriculum itself and in faculty and student responses were evident. The curriculum changed from a subject-centered focus to a student-centered focus, as evidenced through the following movements in attitude:

- From "These are the courses you will get" to "These are the competencies you will be required to demonstrate."

- From "This is the content covered" to "These are the learning experiences provided."

- From "Students should already be able to do this before they get to us" to "How can we accommodate student academic needs?"

- From concern about information presented to concern for the consequences in terms of student growth.

None of the tasks was easy. No curriculum change happened without hardship and pain; as faculty and students began to see the fruits of their labors in improved student and faculty performance, the pain subsided. Attention refocused on nourishing the program and making it work.

CHAPTER 6

FACULTY DEVELOPMENT FOR EXCELLENCE

In addition to the years of negative press, the absence of feelings of control over student achievement on the NTE and over their own destinies had resulted in a battered faculty. Although dedicated and capable, the faculty was in need of (1) a sense of direction, (2) reaffirmation that their efforts with students in classrooms could make a significant difference in student achievement on the NTE and other measures, and (3) assurance that a systematic improvement plan, implemented for long-term improvement and short-range change, could provide the "survival" strategy for which they had been searching.

Most of the faculty realized that change was a necessary ingredient for improving the college's situation; **but** they were unsure as to the nature of the change required. Neither were the faculty members ready for change. Some efforts had to be made to establish the environment from which educational and program improvement change could grow. Realizing that the need for an organized staff development process was great and that the change process would be impeded without it, key administrators in the college employed a systematic approach to faculty development beginning with goals identification.

GOALS OF FACULTY DEVELOPMENT

Faculty development targeted both the affective and cognitive dimensions of faculty renewal. Among the affective goals were (1) to improve faculty morale, (2) to promote feelings of faculty cohesion, and (3) to increase faculty commitment to the efforts necessary to redesign the teacher preparation program. Other goals were tied specifically to the total improvement effort for the teacher education program. These were translated into a series of objectives to promote improvement and included:

- To increase faculty knowledge and skills required for implementation of the redesigned program.

- To increase faculty awareness of current levels of student performance and student competencies required for successful performance.

- To improve course designs and faculty skills in designing course syllabi targeting required student competencies.

- To improve instructional delivery to promote competency development.

- To analyze student performance data and to use the data in course design and/or revision.

- To improve faculty skills in designing relevant instruments to assess student competencies.

- To promote faculty acceptance of accountability for the quality and outcomes of instruction in courses for which individual faculty members were responsible.

- To increase faculty awareness of support resources for use in and beyond the classroom.

- To improve the advisory system.

- To improve faculty abilities to function as team members.

It was anticipated that some affective goals would be addressed by staff development activities focusing on content to enhance faculty knowledge and on methods to increase responsible objectives-oriented instruction. Even so, some staff development sessions would have as primary purposes dealing with faculty unity, faculty commitment, and preparation for the change environment. This was the nature of the first session with the faculty at the beginning of the 1980 school year.

Later faculty development formats included (1) major conferences with nationally recognized consultants making presentations to faculty and students, including, a three-day conference, "Testwiseness for the Culturally Different," featuring Dr. Arthur Whimbey, Dr. Thelma Spencer, and Dr. Charles Gifford; (2) informal faculty brainstorm sessions around specific topics such as means for strengthening student performance in courses and on tests; (3) informal faculty sharing of procedures found effective in promoting student study and self-initiated use of available resources; (4) individual faculty study of available resources and test items from the NTE "dead file;" (5) small-group sessions for peer review of course syllabi; (6) individual study and sharing of NTE vocabulary lists and other study materials developed in-house and those provided by the Educational Testing Service; (7) special problem-solving forums frequently involving the faculty of other similar institutions; and (8) in-house presentations and discussions of new and emerging program features, such as the newly developed program of professional laboratory experiences, with policies and procedures for implementation.

SUBSTANCE FOR FACULTY DEVELOPMENT AND CHANGE

Educational audits, analyses of student achievement, and priorities (goals) set by the faculty provided direction for planning the content for faculty development sessions. These sessions provided the means for promoting the goals and objectives related to the total improvement of the overall teacher education program. Specific faculty development topics and activities follow.

Increasing Skill in Designing Course Syllabi and Instruction. Once sets of skills and competencies were assigned to the specific professional courses as described, the faculty needed to revise all course syllabi to include them. Faculty development activities were designed to facilitate this process. A faculty committee studied, prepared, and submitted for faculty approval a syllabus format to be used for all COE courses. This syllabus outline required that all expected competencies be identified for students by category (College of Education or NTE) and by level (introductory, reinforcement, mastery), and that these be translated into course objectives. The faculty engaged in small- and large-group sessions to provide peer assistance in creating course syllabi that not only specified required competencies to be demonstrated by students before exiting from the course, but also specified appropriate learning activities, evaluative procedures, required readings, and bibliographies.

After faculty members prepared syllabi consistent with the approved standardized format, the syllabi were submitted to a syllabus review team consisting of COE faculty and administrators. Team responsibility included ascertaining that the syllabi (1) were in approved format, (2) included all College of Education and National Teacher Examinations competencies assigned to the specific course, and (3) contained instructional activities and resources clearly related to student development of prescribed competencies. Critiqued syllabi were returned for faculty revisions as necessary.

Increasing Performance Standards Through Improved Instruction. A second aspect of these sets of faculty development activities included designing and implementing instruction with rigorous demands for student performance. Sessions were presented to assist the faculty in designing competency-based professional education and specialized academic education courses. The courses were designed to include not only those activities to take place during class time, but also professional laboratory experiences in the field and supplemental, student-needs-based assistance to be secured in the Education Resource Center.

Important changes in performance standards were facilitated by the COE's newly agreed upon principles and assumptions about the system of teacher education, the apportionment activities, and the course and syllabus design activities. First, faculty members began to understand that what they traditionally considered "their courses" really belonged to the teacher preparation program. The faculty realized that the COE and the system of teacher education itself had a vested interest in the content and conduct of each course. They came to understand that it was within the rights and responsibilities of other involved faculty and administrators to prescribe what should be included in each course. Second, the sense of ownership of courses shifted to a sense of ownership of accountability for student competencies as developed by courses. Concomitantly, faculty demonstrated increased awareness of the role played by each and every course in the overall curriculum and in the development of competent program graduates.

Increasing Skills in Analyzing Performance Data. Consultants from Education Testing Service were invited once a semester during the early stages of program revision and at least once each year subsequently to lead the faculty in analyzing the NTE performance data of College of Education majors. These data were presented by test components and competency clusters within the components. The teacher education faculty, including members from other departments throughout the university were provided with an item analysis of student performance from the most recent testing. This analysis included looking at the questions, COE student responses, and varying rationales for the students' response choices and the correct choices, as well as comparative data for students at other state institutions and on the national level.

These activities resulted in (1) greater faculty accountability for student performance in competence clusters relegated to their courses, (2) increased understanding of curriculum revision needs and revisions in instructional approaches required for improved student performance, and (3) increased familiarity with test item types used by Educational Testing Service to assess a stated competence. These analyses contributed to the data base for curricular decisionmaking as well.

Increasing Skills in Designing Relevant Tests. A series of workshops was designed to enhance faculty test-construction skills because it was believed that training the faculty to develop and regularly administer simulated competency tests within courses would enhance both faculty and student accountability. Test-construction workshops were developed around information provided by Educational Testing Service for preparing NTE-like test items. Faculty members applied their newly acquired skills in preparing NTE-like test items designed to measure competencies assigned to the specific courses each professor taught. These test items were exchanged for peer review and subsequent revision.

The College of Education also participated in the consortium efforts sponsored by the Southern Regional Education Board (SREB), which targeted designing NTE-like items. Also, as a member of the consortium, the college was

81

able to share items created by its faculty and to secure pertinent items created by the faculties of other institutions.

As a result of these efforts, the faculty began to include NTE-like tests in their courses, to use the test data from the instruments as diagnostic tools, and to prescribe Education Resource Center activities as avenues for mastering those competencies in which a student showed weaknesses. The faculty also decided to use items from the NTE-like examinations as learning activities whereby they modeled the thought processes required to select correct responses.

Increasing Skills in Advising Students. Content from faculty workshops and other sessions such as those explaining state certification requirements became content for dissemination to students through the advisement system. Likewise, increasing the effectiveness of the advisory system itself became the content of other faculty development sessions. A number of these departmental-level and collegewide sessions centered on how to use the diagnostic data collected on all education majors in advising students about the program, monitoring of their progress, implementing prescriptive procedures for those showing weaknesses, and building student and faculty accountability for course choices. At other times sessions focused on implementing the newly developed admission and monitoring system.

Outgrowths of the activities included a clearer understanding of the entire improvement program by faculty, improved faculty ability to articulate program features to involved students, and enhanced levels of communication between faculty and advisees, which provided the opportunity for faculty to discuss program requirements and expectations with students. Advisors were more accountable for advisees' progress and seemed to encourage advisees to seek and obtain developmental assistance as indicated on the students' diagnostic profiles. Students realized that they were to be held accountable for competence development and began to behave in more goal-oriented ways.

Increasing Skills in Using New Resources. Addition of resources in the College of Education necessitated staff development activities targeting awareness of the resources, orientation to their use in the teacher education program, and hands-on experiences where the new resources were demonstrated. These new resources were a support system for (1) faculty as they worked toward implementing competency-based professional courses, (2) education students who had needs which could not be met during regular class meetings, and (3) advisors who wanted to assist individual students in securing needed skills (as indicated on the student profiles), but whose workloads precluded individual teaching sessions.

The delivery system for faculty development in this area involved site visits by faculty to nearby facilities that offered assistance to educators in developing computer literacy skills, securing consultants with computer skills to make faculty presentations, and sending interested faculty members to computer workshops. Once the Education Resource Center (ERC) opened, faculty members were able to secure much of the technical training they needed and desired through the ERC staff. Some of the training was pre-scheduled, while other training was scheduled individually.

The outcomes of these activities included increased use of ERC facilities and resources by faculty and students. The faculty, in particular, showed a greater degree of confidence in the support provided by the dean. Also, faculty members supplied course support and enhancement-type materials to ERC staff to be used by students. Much of these materials was placed on microcomputers for student-initiated study.

Achieving Long-Term Results. As stated in the consultant's notes, the COE undertook a long-term arrangement with an outside consultant for faculty and leadership team development. The staff development plan called for a variety of formats ranging from all-day retreats to half-day sessions, from group discussions for airing concerns to formal presentations, from entire faculty involvement to sessions with only leadership teams. Objectives for this set of staff development activities included: assessing needs, preparing for change, building commitment to change, increasing goal-setting skills, sharing success and celebrating accomplishments, accommodating differences in work styles of faculty and leaders, developing and expanding leadership skills, and developing the general organization.

Increasing Productivity and Scholarly Endeavors. Additional to the staff development activities for achieving immediate change in student performance levels were other faculty opportunities for personal and professional growth. To encourage faculty research, professional writing, and other creative activities, the college sponsored specific workshops and granted release time to more than 30 percent of its faculty over the six-year span reported. For example, the college provided release time for faculty to attend locally sponsored workshops to refine their skills in writing proposals for generating resources. The college itself provided external consultants at least once per semester to assist faculty in exploring ideas and providing technical assistance in proposal development.

Increasing Skills in Working as a Team Toward Common Goals. The faculty development program expected changes in the affective domain as well as the cognitive domain, but affective changes were more slowly realized than some of the more tangible goals. The first annual fall retreat in 1980 resulted in the faculty unanimously identifying these items as high priority for immediate attention: (1) preparing students for success on competence measures such as the NTE, and (2) promoting positive images of the college and its programs by promoting quality in the program. The faculty voiced unanimous acceptance of the goals. That was a first step; **but** the distance between accepting common goals and working as a team to accomplish them was great and the path was rough. Working as a team was the most difficult feat of all and may, as yet, be only marginally fulfilled. As is the case with many faculties, Grambling's COE faculty represented varying philosophies, varying degrees of commitment, and varying degrees of resistance to change. The college had those faculty members who adopted the "I'll-stand-back-and-watch-you-fail" attitude; it had other faculty members and administrators determined not to fail. The activities of the latter group began to energize others and to prompt and support other faculty members to give the plan a fair chance by their cooperating and participating.

Resistance to the change in the College of Education was eroded by the evidence that the plan to achieve excellence was effective. As student performance on the National Teacher Examination improved, so did investment of faculty energies in program endeavors. The faculty, through staff development, grew into a team. Team spirit was catalyzed by renewed confidence in self and colleagues, faith in the correctness of the path chosen by the college, belief that given appropriate and intensive instructional experience students could master the program objectives, and a taste of success.

CONSULTANT'S NOTE #4:

CARING FOR AN ORGANIZATION IN TRANSITION

Organizations that are in a transitional state for any duration almost always experience virus-like disorders that disrupt their progress. This is to be expected because expending so much energy to effect change reduces resistance in two areas: the organization's alertness, and mental and physical stamina of the organization's members. For example, people experience various forms of burnout and blurred vision of the desired goal, and the organization's productivity dips frequently.

Grambling's COE was not immune to these problems. During one of my visits, I observed great improvements and I saw the number of students passing the NTE had increased, but I also noticed the sluggishness of the organization. People seemed unaware of the success of their efforts. Lack of follow-through in monitoring the changes had allowed too many things to slip through the cracks: (1) people were losing themselves in details of little import; (2) the college's small cadre of leaders were complaining more than ever, and they were beginning to irritate each other and the management; and (3) although a number of questions still confronted the college, decisionmaking seemed to be in a suspended state–people were unable or unwilling to make decisions that would provide answers to important questions and thus move the organization forward. The kinds of questions that seemed most prominent included the following:

- When can short-term interventions such as tutoring be disengaged or left to manage themselves so that faculty do not have to expend inordinate amounts of energy on them?

- Can the COE graduate identified high-risk students in four years?

- What should be the college's admissions level? Should the college raise its standards?

Clearly, the COE was under attack from within and from the silent foes of inertia and burnout. It must be understood, however, that although productivity was slipping, people were still working and pushing. We concluded from a diagnosis of the situation that the college needed assistance in managing its own motivation. We examined seven intervention factors (Hunter, 1971): (1) concern or degree of tension, (2) interest, (3) feeling tone, (4) perceived success, (5) knowledge of results, (6) intrinsic rewards, and (7) extrinsic rewards.

After careful consideration, the dean decided upon a second retreat for COE faculty. This was to be a morale booster–a celebration session to keep everyone's energy flowing. Without such activities, people have a tendency to be so anxious about the things they are changing, they often fail to look back and use self-satisfaction to generate energy toward continuing success. In addition, this second retreat had a hidden agenda to help the faculty understand, via catharsis-type activities, what the organization was experiencing.

The second retreat began with an activity focused on the college's success. Each department told what it had done that contributed to the improved performance of students, and they identified other successes beyond students' NTE performance. Later the group looked at how to maintain the improved performance levels of students and how to accommodate differences in the working styles of leaders and faculty members.

The faculty's reaction to the session was significantly positive. They responded to acknowledgment of their success with sighs of relief, gigantic smiles, and applause representing their own pats on the back.

All but one of the adjustment factors had been addressed effectively by this short-term activity. The exception was adjustment to the system of extrinsic rewards. This area required more time. Given the dean's word that he would work on improving the reward system, burnout was addressed only minimally on this occasion. Stressing the college's success helped to renew some of the leaders' energies, but it was obvious that the dean would need to expand the leadership team. If the necessary skills were not available in the existing faculty, new people would have to be hired from outside the college.

The process of celebration of achievements and successes has not been completely institutionalized at this point. The organization will need more practice in this area, in my opinion.

CHAPTER 7

MONITORING: STUDENT, FACULTY, AND CHANGE

Qualitative improvements in students' performance on tests and in the teacher education program at Grambling State University is, in part, attributable to a fine-tuned monitoring system. A salient characteristic of this system is that it holds students, faculty, and administrators accountable for performing tasks according to established procedures and within specified times.

The monitoring system was the college's response to the monumental task of blueprinting ways and means to ascertain accountability in teacher education systemwide. Development of the system began with a search for answers to such questions as the following:

- What should a prospective teacher look like and be able to do at incremental stages in his or her professional development?

- What type of activities or checkpoints could be installed to ascertain that students possessed critical behaviors and skills at prescribed stages?

- Who would assume responsibility for validating critical skills?

- What procedures could be installed to monitor and evaluate program changes?

- Once designed, how could the blueprint be operationalized, minimizing anxieties on the part of students and faculty alike?

Extensive initial deliberations by the faculty and the College of Education Council yielded what seemed to be sensible responses to these and other emerging questions surrounding an adequate monitoring system. Such interactions also revealed clearly that the remaining developmental task would be a mammoth undertaking. Beginning with a set of objectives, the council began to operationalize its answers, which gave direction to both the people and the paper activities that were needed to implement a system capable of realizing excellence and accountability in teacher education.

OBJECTIVES OF THE MONITORING SYSTEM

The major purpose of the monitoring system was, and is, to provide a procedural means of assuring that the behavior of students, faculty, administrators, and changes in policies and practices all achieve, in measurable outcomes, the purpose of the COE. This overall purpose was translated into three objectives, one for each constituent—student, faculty, and change.

Students. When monitoring student behavior, the College of Education expected its graduates' performance to be a reliable, consistent, and observable expression of its purposes. The objective is:

> To define, direct, and supervise the activities of students in the teacher preparation program so that the end product is a quality education, defined as proficiency in communication skills; demonstrated possession of a general body of knowledge, reasonable to expect of a well-educated individual; demonstrated knowledge and competence in a minimum of two areas of specialized academic content; a demonstrated body of professional knowledge and entry-level skills for the teaching profession; a bachelor's degree and a regular teaching certificate.

Faculty. The objective of the monitoring system for faculty behavior also was based on specific expectations. Faculty members were expected to provide students with activities. This expectation required them to demonstrate proficiency in communication skills, extended their general knowledge base, and required them to develop agreed upon professional and specialized competences. In addition, faculty advisors were expected to guide, counsel, and serve as mentors to students in ways resulting in students' receiving degrees and teaching certificates. The objective was stated thus:

> To define, direct, and supervise the activities of faculty members so that the measurable results will be documentation of actions contributing to students' proficiency in communication skills; acquisition of a general body of knowledge reasonable to expect of an educated individual; mastery of a body of knowledge and skills in a minimum of two areas of specialization; assimilation of a body of professional knowledge and entry-level skills to the profession; receipt of a bachelor's degree and a teaching certificate.

Change. The objective of the monitoring system applied to change (defined as a systematic approach to internal reform) was also couched in expectations that the COE held for reforms. Change in standards for admission in the COE was expected to provide a number of tangible results. These are specified in the following objective:

To define, direct, and supervise change so that it produces measurable outcomes of its contributions to the students' development of proficiency in communication skills; acquisition of a general body of knowledge reasonable to expect of any well-educated individual; acquisition of a body of knowledge in two areas of specialized academic content; receipt of a bachelor's degree; and receipt of a teaching certificate from the State of Louisiana.

COMPONENTS OF THE SYSTEM

The blueprint for the system called for four major components, each with an identifiable function and specific sets of activities: testing, record keeping, internal/external evaluations, and dissemination of information. Each component, with its specific functions and sample activities, is described below.

Testing. The testing component is designed to assess students' strengths and weaknesses according to specific program standards. Testing activities are incorporated at key points in the program and for the following specific purposes:

1. On application for admission to the COE, testing activities are initiated for each candidate. The objective is to collect data to help determine the extent to which applicants possess basic communication skills, and the general knowledge that one might expect of a high school graduate. Specifically, this determination is made by administering and interpreting the results of applicants' performances on the COE Mathematics Proficiency Examination, the COE English Proficiency Examination, the Sequential Test of Educational Progress (STEP), the ACT or SAT, and the Nelson-Denny Reading Test.

   Based on the results, applicants' strengths and weaknesses are identified. This knowledge is used to prescribe a remedial educational program for students who need assistance in developing skills prerequisite to unconditional admission. In-house remedial and tutorial services are provided to prospective teacher education majors with potential who show skill weaknesses and to whom the COE has made commitments for their development as quality candidates for teaching programs.

2. On application to a teaching program, students again must undergo or present evidence of having successfully completed the general knowledge and the communication skills modules of the NTE core battery.

Although not a pencil-paper test, a departmental interview indicates other criteria desirable for a professional: evidence of commitment to teaching; ability to communicate well orally; evidence of social and emotional maturity; and evidence of good interpersonal skills. Applicants must "pass" the interview by being recommended by the screening committee for program admission.

3. After applicants are admitted to a teaching program, several testing activities occur: (a) Students must take the pre- and post-departmental test of professional and subject field knowledge during their sophomore, junior, and senior years. (b) Before completing the advanced methods course, required of all majors, students must pass the third module of the NTE core battery, the professional knowledge module. The course is recommended as a first-semester, senior-year offering. (c) Students must meet the criterion score on the appropriate speciality area component of the NTE before they complete student teaching.

4. At the point of program exit, degree candidates must pass a departmental comprehensive examination.

Other testing activities are interspersed throughout the program. These include NTE-like examinations prepared and administered by the individual professors of professional courses, NTE-like examinations developed for computer-assisted learning, and NTE-like examinations that are pencil-paper activities used in COE testwiseness initiatives. These activities are used to diagnose and evaluate students and to familiarize them with and sensitize them to the content demands and structural characteristics of competence measures such as the NTE.

Outcomes of the testing component contribute to the intent and purpose of the admissions and monitoring system. Assessment data (1) facilitate use of multiple measures of personal and professional characteristics, including proficiency in basic skills; (2) provide information to support student advisement such as design and implementation of remediation plans, scheduling of professional courses, recommendations of self-help study, tutorial services, or both, readiness assessment for successful completion of NTE modules, etc.; (3) provide baseline information for measuring students' progress and determining their readiness for advancement to the next program stage; and (4) support a systematic approach to assisting potentially capable students who have professional and personal deficiencies in developing prerequisite competencies needed for survival in the mainstream curriculum and for success as a teacher.

Record Keeping. Critical to the smooth operation of the system, immediate access to relevant data on student personnel in a format that is useful and easily interpreted is provided by the record-keeping component. These data are important not only to the advisement process, but also in the decision-making process at key points in the student's progress–eligibility for admission to the College of Education; eligibility for admission to a teaching program; eligibility for admission to advanced standing; eligibility for advanced methods; eligibility for admission to student teaching; eligibility for admission to the senior comprehensive examination; and eligibility for graduation and certification or licensure.

Data collection activities involve all procedures through which vital information on students' performance and involvement is gathered. These include securing the following:

- copies of students' transcripts

- individual student scores on the ACT or SAT, STEP, and Nelson-Denny from the University Testing Center or the COE Testing Center

- individual copies of student NTE scores

- computer printouts of students' involvement in remedial, tutorial, and self-improvement activities under the supervision of personnel in the Educational Resource Center (ERC).

To facilitate data collection for record-keeping purposes, standard forms are used to make requests for transcripts from the campus registrar, test scores from the University Testing Center, remedial involvement of students in the ERC, and for other pertinent data from the student.

Data-recording activities include preparing a profile and folder for each applicant seeking admission to the college. The student profile presents, in convenient form, all pertinent data on students. In addition, the record-keeping component records summary-type data and comparative group data on students.

Data accessibility activities make data readily available to administrators and faculty who need this confidential information. Complete data sets on each student are available in the department in which the student is majoring, the student's advisors' office, and the COE's Office of Student Services (subsequently renamed CARE Center–Centralized Advisement, Referral and Evaluation Center). At present, the COE is working to convert the data bases to computers for greater convenience and accessibility.

Internal/External Evaluation Component. The internal/external evaluation component of the monitoring system provides a means of measuring the reliability and consistency of students' performances on both in-house and standardized instruments designed to assess the presence of specified competencies. Internal evaluation occurs, for example, when the college administers its in-house

COE English Proficiency Examination, the COE Math Proficiency Examination, and the Nelson Denny Reading Test, departmental tests, and NTE-simulated tests. To determine the extent to which instructors are helping students to master the competencies that have been assigned to respective courses, someone other than the course instructor administers NTE-simulated tests.

Another form of internal evaluation is the practice of appointing a faculty member within each department to serve as the internal monitor. The monitor's responsibility is to evaluate the extent to which the department has achieved its established and approved goals for the academic year. Always among these goals is one that focuses on recruitment and admission.

Several activities are pursued to secure input on total program effectiveness and the effectiveness of individual program components—for example: (1) During the eight-year improvement effort, the College of Education underwent two self-studies and external audits from accrediting and certification agencies—the National Council for Accreditation of Teacher Education (NCATE) and the Louisiana State Department of Education. The NCATE audit provided program confirmation through reaccreditation. Program approval was derived from the State Department of Educations' audit. (2) An official from ETS, Dr. Thelma Spencer, spent several days on-site documenting and evaluating program components. (3) At the dean's request, a Blue Ribbon Committee, comprised of professionals throughout the university's service area, evaluated the effectiveness of the Professional Laboratory Experiences Program itself and its attendant policies and procedures. Reports from these efforts provided additional evaluative data for subsequent action steps.

Another external evaluation activity consisted of establishing external evaluation committees to document and evaluate individual department attainment of stated yearly goals. Each department prepared a yearly list of goals and objectives corresponding to those generated through the dean's office. In large measure, these related to improving the programs, upgrading students' entry- and exit-level skills and their subsequent performance on competence measures, and generating resources. The evaluation committees prepared reports for the department and the dean.

Dissemination of Information Component. Information is vital to a monitoring system because it empowers administrators, faculty, and students to take informed action. To disseminate information, the COE frequently conducts many activities, primarily to provide students with information to support their personal and professional goals. Information largely is delivered by faculty presentations and by department and collegewide meetings. Faculty members meet their advisees weekly for 50 minutes as a whole group and for shorter periods with students one-on-one. In these settings, faculty advisors keep students abreast of program requirements, admission requirements, academic requirements, and in general, everything students need to know about their programs of study, whether they ask or not.

Department and collegewide meetings are held at least twice each year. Information in classes is reinforced at these meetings. Additionally, it is at these meetings that major changes in policies and procedures that affect students' admission and academic development are presented to students. The format for these meetings permits students to make comments and raise questions.

Data on student performance as a group are disseminated on a regular basis to the faculty. These reports not only serve to assist advisors, but also provide data bases for decisions regarding effectiveness or ineffectiveness of courses, remedial and enrichment opportunities, and the admissions and monitoring system itself. These data provide the continuous "pulse rate" of the total program.

PEOPLE AND PAPER ACTIVITIES: WHO DOES WHAT AND WHEN?

The admissions and monitoring system requires a carefully sequenced plan of systematic student progress checkpoints validated by many different people. As would be expected, the roles and responsibilities also are carefully worked out to promote effective functioning of the monitoring system.

Members of the faculty, administrators, and the Office of Student Services (CARE) perform distinct roles in the admission process, defined as all activities involved in getting students to the university, to the college, to a program, to courses, to graduation, and to certification. Faculty roles include advisor and instructor. In the advisory role, faculty members keep records of and monitor students' progress from the time they are admitted to the COE through their meeting certification and graduation requirements. This includes advising students to apply for admission to a program by the end of their sophomore year; to admission to advanced standing and to advanced methods by the end of their junior year; and to student teaching by the end of the first semester of the senior year. Throughout students' programs, faculty advisors review students' strengths and weaknesses, presenting and discussing with students their performance data, suggesting any remedial steps to be taken, assessing student readiness for success on required standardized measures and advising students on scheduling various tests. They also advise students of their needs to take required or remedial courses.

Documentation of advisement is handled by advisors completing with students an NCR-type curriculum contract with appropriate comments. Both the student and the advisor must sign a contract. Copies are then sent to each of these persons, the department head, and the Student Services Office.

Faculty advisors also serve as members of departmental screening committees who interview students as a part of the procedure for admitting students to programs. If students do not meet admission-level criteria, faculty advisors assist their advisees in developing and implementing alternate plans that lead to meeting the specified and published admission standards.

The role of instructor requires faculty members to assume responsibility for protecting the academic credibility of the curriculum. To this end, they monitor students' eligibility for admission to specific courses. Instructors must ask students who do not meet specified admission criteria to remove themselves from courses. Course eligibility is explained in greater detail in a later section of this chapter.

Administrators play a significant role in academic admissions monitoring. Department heads frequently review the files of students who have not applied for admission to various levels and provide critical information to students and their advisors. When students apply for admission and meet admission criteria, department heads schedule the interviews that departmental committees conduct. Students are notified of the date, time, and place of their respective admission interview by the department head. If students do not meet admission criteria, they are informed and given the reason(s) why they cannot be admitted at that point. They are also advised about what they need to do to become eligible. (Copies of forms facilitating these functions are included in the Appendix.)

In addition, department heads prepare department files on applicants to be interviewed and make them available to the chairpersons of the admission committees. An applicant's file includes his or her transcript, curriculum sheet on which grades have been recorded for courses completed, application for admission to a program, student profile, a guide for the admission interview, and an admission contract. The latter is executed for students who are eligible for admission, but whose oral interview, writing sample, ACT and SAT scores indicate that they could profit from some tutorial and self-help activities.

The Office of Student Services also plays an important role in the admissions and monitoring system. This office monitors the overall admission and monitoring process for the COE and maintains files for each student. These data are applied to admissions criteria and the director makes recommendations for (1) admission to the COE, (2) conditional admission to the COE, or (3) denial of admission. The office receives and disseminates to respective departments each student's applications for admission to a teaching program, although action on the application is initiated by the respective department. The office is also responsible for collecting data on students, disseminating relevant data to other offices and to students, and forming an external tier of monitoring. This activity includes receiving student applications for various monitoring points from departments, examining them in light of criteria and standards, validating relevant data, and forwarding student records to the dean, department heads, or both.

MORE THAN A PAPER TRAIL

The admissions and monitoring system does require paper-pencil activities and broad dissemination of data, but it is not a paper system. The paper trail is a by-product of a complete, functional system emerging from the college's need to keep abreast of all aspects of the program at all times. The system provides ready answers to such critical questions as:

- How are our students performing on the COE English Proficiency Test? Any module of the NTE?

- What does the profile on a typical student look like at application for COE admission? Program admission? Application for student teaching?

- How does the typical student profile differ, for example, in 1987 from 1980?

- What program differences correspond to changes in student performance?

- Are some students slipping through cracks. If so, what procedures can prevent it?

The admissions and monitoring system underwent several stages of evaluation before arriving at its present form as described here. The procedures for admission and monitoring students currently involve six steps or levels of admission.

1. **Admission to the College of Education.** Formal applications are filed by the student and evaluated along with other data by the Office of Student Services for evidences of eligibility which include:

   - Completion of prescribed courses in the College of Basic Studies and Services

   - Formal application for transfer from the College of Basic Studies and Services

   - Formal application for Admission to the College of Education

   - A minimum grade-point average of 2.0 on a 4.0 scale

- Demonstrated proficiency in communication skills as evidenced by

  a. minimum grade-level score of 11.0 on a standardized reading test

  b. minimum score of 125 on the 180-item COE English Proficiency Test (140 minimum after fall 1986)

  c. a "pass" evaluation on the required essay portion of the COE English Proficiency Test

- A minimum score of 80 percent accuracy on the COE Mathematics Proficiency Test

- A minimum grade of *C* in the first professional course: Ed. 162, Introduction to Teaching

- Evidence of completion of a minimum of 15 clock hours of observation and participation in public school classrooms comprised of students from varied socioeconomic and ethnic backgrounds

Students who meet the prescribed standards may be eligible for full admission. If, however, the student has a deficiency in one or more of the tested areas, he or she may be recommended for conditional admission. This status must be changed by the end of two semesters with the presentation of required test scores or other documentation of proficiency to the Office of Student Services.

2. **Admission to a Teaching Program.** Students planning to pursue a teacher preparation program must meet specific requirements.

- Unconditional admission to the COE

- Formal application for admission to a teaching program

- Minimum GPA of 2.5 on a 4.0 scale

- Criterion performance on two modules of the NTE core battery: communication skills and general knowledge

- Minimum grade of *C* in all English courses

- Recommendation based on a formal interview with the departmental screening committee

The formal interview conducted by at least a two-member faculty screening committee is designed to glean data unavailable about the applicant through tests. These include interpersonal skills, ability to express ideas well in an oral setting, responses under pressure, evidence of commitment to teaching, motivation toward scholarly activity, and other personal characteristics. Also involved in the process is the requirement that the applicant write an essay of at least four paragraphs in response to a given stimulus statement or question. The committee considers the content and form of this product in its ratings of the applicant. Recommendations from each screening committee are sent for approval to the department head who then transfers the applications to the Office of Student Services for a final check of eligibility.

3. **Admission to Professional Education Courses.** A recent addition to the monitoring process is the restriction of students pursuing courses in the professional education sequence. Students who have not been admitted to the College of Education are eligible to pursue only 100- and 200-level professional education courses. Enrollment in 300-level professional courses is limited to those students admitted to the COE and to a teaching program. Professional courses at the 400 level are restricted to students admitted to the COE, a teaching program, and advanced standing. These restrictions not only protect the integrity of the courses, but also prohibit students from taking courses out of the prescribed sequence and before they have the prerequisites for success in the courses.

4. **Admission to Advanced Standing.** To be admitted to advanced standing, students must meet the following criteria.

- Full admission to the COE

- Full admission to a teaching program

- Completion of all freshman- and sophomore-level courses with a minimum GPA of 2.5

- Completion of the English sequence with a minimum grade of *C* in each course

- Completion of each professional and specialized academic course with a minimum grade of *C*

- Formal application completed and filed with the department head

- Completion of a minimum of 40 observation and participation hours validated by the Office of Professional Laboratory Experiences

- Acceptable scores on departmental pre- and post-tests and the NTE

- Recommendations from advisor and department head

5. **Admission to Advanced Methods.** Students who have achieved admission at all other preceding points may be eligible for admission to advanced methods courses by meeting additional criteria:

- Proficiency in communicative skills

- Exemplary moral and ethical character

- Freedom from handicapping conditions that would interfere with teaching effectiveness

- Recommendations from advisor(s), department head, and dean

- Completion of required reading methods sequence

- Completion of all 200- and 300-level professional courses

- A minimum grade of *C* in each professional course taken

- Appropriate scores on the NTE and departmental examinations

- A formal application

- Approval by advisor and department head

6. **Admission to Student Teaching.** Those students, admitted at all preceding levels, may be admitted to student teaching with these requirements:

- Satisfactory completion of all freshman-, sophomore- and junior-level courses with a minimum GPA of 2.5

- Demonstration of social and emotional maturity

- Exemplary moral and ethical character

- Completion of observation-participation requirement of a minimum 100 hours

- General proficiency in communication skills

- Freedom from handicapping conditions that would interfere with effective teaching

- Satisfactory completion of advanced methods courses

- Recommendation from advisor(s) and department head

- Completion of NTE professional knowledge module with required score

Student applications are screened in the Office of Professional Laboratory Experiences and forwarded to respective departments for action. For secondary majors, excluding those in health and physical education, approval must be granted by both professional and academic liaison advisors.

7. **Eligibility for Graduation**. Students who complete all program requirements may be eligible for graduation provided they meet these additional requirements:

- Minimum GPA of 2.5

- Completion of appropriate NTE specialty area test with required score

- Pass score on senior comprehensive

- Formal application

CONCLUDING PERSPECTIVE

These carefully structured procedures were not designed to exclude or eliminate candidates from the teaching pool. Rather the admissions and monitoring system has provided the college with opportunities to work with students, faculty, and administrators; to cultivate students who are competent professionals at the end of their programs, regardless of their entry-level skills. The procedures have fostered accountability for student progress and performance by all involved: administrators, faculty, and students. The system has exacted peak performance from the same role groups. Perhaps some students still fall through the cracks and get through the program with less than their best performances, **but** unquestionably they are fewer now than before implementation of the system.

CHAPTER 8

THE DEANSHIP:

MAJOR PROBLEMS CONFRONTING LEADERSHIP FOR ACADEMIC EXCELLENCE

Under normal circumstances, people may not expect much from a college dean, but during periods of educational reform, college deans are expected to make things happen, to make a difference. These expectations were in place for the new dean of Grambling's College of Education in 1980. The president and the vice president for academic affairs made it clear that the low test performance of teacher education graduates on the NTE had to improve. They needed management from the dean that would advance the college's growth and productivity. This chapter, an adventure in administrative reflection, explains some of the outstanding problems and issues in addressing this situation and the significant actions taken to bring about positive outcomes.

The concept of excellence in teacher education appears to be an uncomplicated notion; the quest for excellence and the achievement thereof, however, are quite complex. These present numerous enigmatic, issue-filled problems that necessarily demand getting hundreds of organizational elements to interlock and operate smoothly and efficiently.

From the perspective of the deanship, the approach to solving Grambling's problems was based on the philosophy that the Dean of Education should assume systemwide leadership in ascertaining that a solution to the problem of poor student performance be addressed and in helping the organization to overcome any inertia which might have set in. Several ancillary beliefs also supported this basic administrative philosophy and motivated administrative action to make things happen. They were that management of reform must:

1. be visionary, keeping the whole picture in sight at all times, under all circumstances.

2. provide leadership, especially in circumstances where management does not control.

3. "hustle" within and outside the college to stay abreast of and, in some cases, ahead of academic happenings that relate to and impinge upon current change efforts.

4. represent an academic entrepreneurship, seeking both economic and academic gains.

5. acknowledge and build upon the college's past successes.

6. squelch feelings of timidity and promote adventuresome, risk-taking, and daring leaders within the college organization.

Application of this philosophy began with the dean's attempt to resolve issues in what seemed to be three critical areas: determining discrepancies between real and perceived problems (i.e., clarifying issues), motivating faculty members and other administrators to desire change, and obtaining and developing material and human resources. Many of these areas probably are of concern in most change efforts at most institutions, and all but one or two potentially success-threatening issues usually can be resolved at the outset. For Grambling, the story was quite different. There were no such administrative discounts; neither were there blueprints for achieving issue resolutions.

UNIFYING VISIONS OF THE PROBLEM AND ITS SOLUTIONS

Informal observations uncovered a discrepancy between what the faculty and the central administration saw as the college's major problem. Many of the faculty saw the problem as a lack of supplies, equipment, and travel monies. The poor performance of the students on the NTE seemed to be a secondary problem that they thought existed because of the poor quality of entering students and the failure of other academic units to do their job. Central administration, on the other hand, believed the problem was the poor performance of the students on the NTE. They thought the situation could be bettered by improving management and faculty productivity within the College of Education.

This perceptual mismatch between the central administration and the faculty presented the new dean with a challenging situation: the discrepancy could lead to ineffectual, random efforts to improve student performance if it were not adequately addressed. A first task for the dean was to discover the origins of the faculty's perception and deal with the discrepancy. Probing unearthed two norms that the college had adopted over the years. The first can be called the "ostrich norm," meaning that the college practiced ignoring or explaining away real problems to hide the perceived deficiencies of the organization and of some organization members. The second, "stockpiling," nurtured the first. The stockpiling norm described the college's practice of accumulating rather than using collected data on students and faculty for program improvement. Similarly, the college was adept at expanding and sensationalizing past and minute contemporary accomplishments, so that outsiders did not look beyond superficial evidence and faculty members were lulled into a false sense of "all-is-well" security. It is ironic that many members came to believe in and worked to protect the somewhat false self-image that the college had developed.

Knowledge of these two norms had significant impact on the administrative approach to eliminate discrepant views of the problem. It motivated (1) presentation of the problem in terms of objective or concrete (statistical) course and student performance data, (2) use of consultants from outside the university who were skilled in organization analysis and development, and (3) removal of the faculty from the physical and psychological environment that represented the old norms to a neutral, temporary environment while attempting to establish new norms and define the problem.

Because matters of reform seemed to cultivate short memories among those undergoing reform at Grambling, unifying the views of the problem of student performance and clarifying the goals for reform were not one-time events. The dean had to remain alert and conduct reaffirmation activities whenever people began to stray from goal-oriented behavior.

INCREASING FACULTY AND ADMINISTRATOR MOTIVATION

At least 70 percent of the academic preparation of teacher education candidates at Grambling is obtained in academic departments outside the College of Education. It was, therefore, important early in the dean's tenure to get the president, vice president, deans, department heads, and faculty in other colleges (Liberal Arts and Sciences) to realize that the poor performance of teacher education students on the NTE was a universitywide problem and that everyone was accountable for planned improvement efforts.

The belief is that no substantive, lasting progress can be made in improving of teacher education in an institution until the president of the institution is visibly involved and strongly committed. This same kind of involvement and commitment must be echoed by the vice president of academic affairs. These individuals must be willing to invest financial and human resources into improvement efforts, investments that are often difficult for historically and predominantly Black college and universities, given their usually limited financial resources. There can be no substitute for such commitment, involvement, and investment, considering the critical minority teacher shortage. As Norman Francis (1986) president of Xavier University reminded, "The next crisis in American public education will be a shortage of minority teachers who can inspire minority students in urban areas to perform as well as their peers in affluent suburbs." Francis lamented, "We have lost one generation in terms of education, and I am afraid we are going to lose another."

From all appearances in 1980, Grambling's College of Education and the other support units were in a heated battle against organizational inertia, especially as it related to education majors. A disappointing number of people seemed content with past accomplishments and complacent about the current state of affairs. They seemed unmoved by the many factors having impact upon teacher education that were changing around them and unconcerned that they too would need to change if Grambling's COE were to regain its status as a leader and remain current and responsive to dynamic societal demands.

Although the ostrich norm might have been operating for some, it seemed unlikely that an entire university would have fallen victim to its malaise. Thus three relevant questions grew out of the dean's observations. (1) Had people become so overwhelmed by the odds they perceived to be against them that they had lost the hope of winning and, consequently, their motivation to try? (2) Considering the average age and extensive number of tenured faculty in the College of Education, had they lost their fear of failure and simply were not trying to be productive? (3) Was it that people had exhausted their ideas for improving student performance and needed new leadership?

An answer to the third question, in part, would seem to be yes, because a new dean had been hired from outside the university. The first two questions, however, demanded additional study. Findings from informal chats, formal surveys, and faculty development sessions revealed that faculty attitudes could be sorted into all three categories represented by the questions. They also suggested the following organizational needs: (1) changing the College of Education from being a near-closed system to being a system open to new ideas and guidance from outside its boundaries; (2) offering renewal activities for tenured faculty members who were either burned out, unmotivated, or retired on the job; (3) reviving the college by introducing innovations; (4) hiring, when possible, new faculty with new ideas; (5) freeing the faculty to say, "I don't know," or "I need help;" (6) providing growth opportunities for tenured faculty motivated toward personal and professional development goals, and (7) providing daily guidance and leadership for faculty members who demonstrated a lack of self-direction.

The dean addressed these needs through a variety of activities. A long-term consultant was brought in periodically to work with the faculty. Self-assessment, personal goal setting, unity and mutual agreement on organizational goals and training were among the areas covered. Along with the consultant's activities, efforts were made to increase opportunities for faculty members to become involved in decision making and to accept more responsibility for initiating and managing reform activities. Persons who demonstrated leadership and growth potential, but who previously were assigned only teaching responsibilities, were given

103

responsibility for special projects, such as chairing various committees, developing the college's marketing and recruiting campaigns, assisting in writing proposals, and designing special student services and events. A third activity to motivate faculty was the development and dissemination of a college newsletter. Its purpose was threefold: to increase the research and writing productivity of faculty members, to provide a means for recognizing and rewarding faculty accomplishments (since financial rewards were minimal), and to initiate a national campaign to turn the college's negative image into a positive one.

Staff development to enhance faculty skills, as described in Chapter Six, represented the fourth response. Administrative efforts consisted largely of finding creative ways on a shoestring budget of bringing consultants to campus to work with faculty. Creativity in this instance consisted of appealing to the volunteerism of some consultants, the benevolence of some technical assistance agencies and trade-offs in expertise and favors with colleagues. Much to the college's benefit, many individuals, organizations, and institutions were eager to give assistance when a sincere plea was made and the college's efforts explained. Finding these opportunities was probably the most difficult part of the reform task, but active involvement in national activities and administrative networking helped the dean to attain a next to impossible feat.

Influencing the support of central administration was much easier than motivating the faculty and administrators across campus to support the college's efforts. Through trial and error, however, it became obvious that the second would follow easier as a function of the first. This linear approach (together with the presentation of concrete data, frequent communication of plans and progress, and the assistance of the long-term consultant) proved to be a successful strategy for winning the support of both constituencies.

MOVING FROM PIPE DREAMS TO BUDGETARY REALITIES

One of the greatest challenges facing the college was acquiring financial resources to fuel the reform necessary to achieve excellence in teacher education. The human reality of "excellence" is as much a matter of money as it is anything else. Although the need for additional funds was not a surprise, it became painfully clear after about a month of study that the College was without adequate resources to deal productively with the problems it faced. Money was needed to actualize its dream. Experience indicates that good leadership, impressive efforts, and good ideas have failed because of a lack of funds. Money cannot save a bad plan and is no substitute for the lack of leadership, but one is grossly mistaken to think quality teacher education is cheap. The belief was and remains that quality teacher education is a high-cost item.

The decision to move early on budget matters was based specifically upon these conditions:

1. The College of Education had a bare-bones budget, too few faculty with skills in needed areas, inadequate teaching supplies, and little or no money for travel.

2. Funds for academic interventions such as remediation would have to come from somewhere other than the existing budget.

3. Faculty morale was acutely low.

4. The college seemed to have little obvious expertise, interest or both to support aggressive pursuit of external funds.

Of the resources the college had on hand to increase the budget, a small cadre of faculty and the dean appeared to offer the most hope for completing the herculean fund-raising task confronting the college. This cadre had to work hard, violate the cultural norms of the environment, dream dreams, and force things to happen. With some training and administrative support, this work group successfully accomplished: (1) researching and identifying potential funding sources, (2) writing and producing proposals, (3) making personal contacts with representatives of potential funding agencies, (4) making recommendations for priortized funding and the economical use of funds, and (5) training other faculty members to assist in writing proposals.

By the end of the second year of pursuing external funds, the college had acquired approximately $250,000 to support its reform efforts. The dean then had the task of managing these financial resources while still seeking others to achieve optimum results. Several measures were taken to ensure such outcomes: prioritizing areas of need for funding, sharing funds for travel, supplies, and equipment among departments, and sharing resources after purchases were made.

In addition to grants, the dean used other methods to acquire resources. For example, the college established an alumni association and appealed through it for financial support. The dean initiated a million-dollar fund-raising campaign, and local businesses were approached for funds to equip and furnish an Education Resource Center. Beyond these projects, academic departments within the college were required to show in their yearly goals and objectives the specific number of dollars they would bring into the college through grants and solicited donations.

In support of efforts to supplement the budget, the dean sponsored subscriptions to literature from government and private funding agencies and disseminated the material among faculty members. Certain calls for proposals were marked and called to the attention of specific persons for follow-up work. Other documents simply had relevant information underlined to help faculty members zero-in on important items. The university's grants administrator also supported the college's efforts. As new information on funds became available, announcements and summaries, along with deadlines for submission of proposals, were shared with everyone. Finally, College of Education faculty members were encouraged to participate in proposal writing workshops sponsored by the college, the university, and other agencies. These efforts and their bountiful outcomes continue–eight years after their initiation.

ANCILLARY PROBLEMS AND PITFALLS

With the problems of definition, motivation, and financial resources more under control, the remaining problems that confronted the college began to loom less ominous and less hopeless. Yet, they represented impediments to change and reform that had to be removed. Some of these ancillary problems and pitfalls include:

1. **Time.** The dean had to prioritize and set aside time to travel and make the program visible nationally. This task would help reverse the college's negative image and develop its identity as a producer of quality teachers. Time also had to be carved out to work with special task forces on writing proposals and planning and monitoring reform activities. Moreover, time was needed to solve people problems. Finally, the dean had to be active in staff development sessions with the faculty. These additions to the administrative schedule were above and beyond those regular duties of the deanship. There never seemed to be enough time to do everything that needed to be done, despite a continuous daylight-to-midnight schedule.

2. **Tradition.** Administrative philosophy and style dictated leaving in place those practices from the past that seemed effective and changing only those practices that had proved to be outdated and ineffective. Yet, this was not enough for some faculty members who had worked through both systems. The dean was constantly plagued by those who desired a return to traditional practices, structures, and sociocultural lifeways within the college organization. Tradition as an impediment to reform transcended the College of Education. These blocks were met across the entire campus and required constant attention.

3. **Burnout.** When organizational reform for excellence rests disproportionately upon the shoulders of a few for any prolonged period, burnout is inevitable. From time to time, beginning about

year three of the improvement program, leaders in the college fell victim to this ailment. It was the dean's responsibility to remain alert for such attacks, provide sources of relief, and ensure that reform efforts continued.

4. **Follow-through.** A large part of the dean's monitoring responsibilities involved making sure that faculty members followed through on assigned projects, newly implemented procedures, and revised curriculum and instructional strategies. For various reasons it seemed much too easy for some faculty to return to old habits or to set their own priorities and not complete goal-oriented tasks. Visits by the dean, progress reports by department heads, and other measures facilitated follow-through. Faculty seemed weakest in this area on matters of student advisement and implementation of remediation strategies.

5. **Professional jealousy and in-house fighting.** As was to be expected, professional jealousies developed among faculty members who perceived that the small cadre of leaders within the college were privy to a special relationship with the dean. They also resented some assignments given to the leaders and felt threatened by the leaders' ability to produce results. Open displays of hostilities and the ignoring or sabotaging of the work of leaders frequently tended to get in the way of progress. Moral and authoritative support for these leaders was a must. Conflict resolution, which preserved the self-respect of everyone, was a process the dean often used.

TOTALITY OF EFFORT

Machiavelli warned in the sixteenth century, "There is nothing more difficult to take in hand, more perilous to conduct or more certain in its success, than to take the lead in the introduction of a new order of things." The problems and pitfalls the college experienced support this perception. Reflecting on the totality of efforts to institute effective and substantive reform, the most difficult part for the dean and others in the college was trying to deal with the impediments of change. Possibly, this was to be expected.

Experience confirms, nonetheless, that leadership still must be visible, consistent, and comprehensive. The education faculty expect the dean to provide leadership. They also expect to be given opportunities to participate in decisions on curriculum and other significant college-related matters. What is to be taught, how standards are to be met, and the nature of the college's mission and goals are among the key decision points for involving faculty. Yet, the ultimate responsibility for the college rests with the dean. If for any reason faculty members fail to act on any significant matters regarding the college, the dean cannot abdicate responsibilities for the consequences.

Grambling's reform efforts continue to be a challenge, but require substantially less energy to cope with today than they did eight years ago. The taste of success, no matter how little, seems to make tasks much easier to achieve.

CHAPTER 9

PROGRESS:

PROGRAM OUTCOMES AND LESSONS LEARNED

How has Grambling's teacher education program changed as a result of improvement efforts? What new information or strategies can Grambling share to help other institutions improve their programs? These and similar questions have been asked since the public announcements of Grambling's accomplishments. This closing chapter summarizes some of the information presented earlier and offers additional illumination of critical program elements that might be important to those interested in replicating the Grambling model. A simplified chart shows before and after program descriptions, and the College's Admissions and Monitoring Checklist for teaching majors (see the Appendix) further clarifies program outcomes in terms of the new steps students are required to take toward completion of a teaching degree. The checklist also indicates the various standards established for student performance at each step.

HOW GRAMBLING'S PROGRAM HAS CHANGED

Because of Grambling's program improvement efforts, change is evident in the teacher training program, in the organizational characteristics of the College of Education, in the university's support of teacher education, and in the attitudes and behaviors of people. Most of these changes are summarized in Table 10.

TABLE 10

IMPACT OF GRAMBLING'S MODEL ON ITS TEACHER EDUCATION PROGRAM

Before	After
A. Organizational Variables	**A. Organizational Changes**
1. Two Departments. Teacher Education and Health, Physical Education and Recreation.	1. Installed three departments: Teacher Education; Health, Physical Education and Recreation; and Educational Leadership and Habilitative Services.
2. Traditional Program Units. Administration, Instruction, and Student Teaching.	2. Restructured and expanded traditional program units by adding early observation/participation experiences, student services office, Educational Resource Center, including tutorial services.
3. Expectations for Organizational Units. Mission of the college was obsolete leading to indefinite goals and behavior.	3. Made definite expectations for organizational units through the development and making public of relevant goals and objectives annually. Yearly evaluations of each unit's accomplishments fostered accountability.
4. Responsibility for Teacher Education. The perception universitywide was that the COE had total responsibility for improving teacher education; that only improvements in professional education were necessary	4. Redefined university responsibility and accountability to teacher education majors with specific emphasis on achieving new standards set in general knowledge areas and instruction and advisement by support colleges.
B. Curriculum Changes	**B. Curriculum Changes**
1. Theoretical/Philosophical Base. Rigidly perceived lines of demarcation in responsibilities that COE and support units have to teaching majors.	1. Sought COE impact upon the total education of preservice teachers, including supervising and assisting in developing their competency in the basic skills areas. Traditional fragmentation of teacher training left too much to chance until support units could be made accountable. The new philosophy also addressed the following: •Definition of a competent teacher

and teaching
•Cognitive/affective needs of teachers.

2. Diagnostic/Remedial Services. Left to universitywide Developmental/ Counseling/Testing Program.

2. Implemented a diagnostic/remediation component within COE that provides student profiles, academic monitoring systems, accountability courses, tutorials, and opportunities for student-initiated assistance. This component allows the college to take a preventive rather than reactive approach to remediation and facilitates successful exit from the program.

3. Clinical Experiences and Field Training. Primarily student teaching with less than desirable opportunities for early field experiences. There was little relationship between instructional program and clinical program.

3. Designed and implemented early observation/participation program beginning in the freshman year. Observation requirements also were attached to critical courses through the senior year. Student teaching seminars were redesigned to incorporate special NTE and testwiseness content.

4. Requirements in General and Professional Knowledge. Existing requirements closely adhered to state requirements for content but greatly exceeded the State in hourly requirements, implying that more of the same would improve performance.

4. Altered course requirements in general and professional knowledge by adding, deleting, and redesigning courses.
•Changed emphasis in part of the English sequence to place more emphasis on writing.
•Changed course requirements to include second phase of U.S. history, and to give more emphasis to humanities and world civilization. Moved to a higher level of math (college algebra) for all programs.
•Changed the focus of science to include botany and zoology and a physical science instead of general science–same 12 hours just changed nature of requirements.
•Installed general education seminar and greater accountability for the mastery of general education content.
•Designed and installed Ed. 162 (Foundations and exploration of teaching as a potential career) for for freshmen students.
•Added junior level course: Philosophical and Sociological Foundations of Education (reinforcement, observation/participation experiences).

C. Changes in People

1. Faculty

   a. Skill Development. Faculty members demonstrated a need to enhance their skills in several areas toward improving the teacher training program.

   b. Attitudes. Faculty members communicated low expectations for student performance, seemed unsure of students' potential for success, felt defeated about preparing students for teacher competency tests, blamed everyone but themselves for students' poor performance, and discouraged students to take teacher tests.

   c. Instruction. Faculty members' course syllabi showed little consideration for basic skills and NTE content. Nor did they have thorough knowledge of what their colleagues in the COE were teaching or of how their instruction related to that of their colleagues. They administered poorly constructed teacher-made tests that reflected a lack of attention to NTE content in instruction and NTE test item formats.

   d. Advisement. Traditional advisement by the COE began with the students' junior year and focused largely upon the professional education sequence,

C. Changes in People

1. Faculty

   a. Through faculty development activities, gained additional skills in test construction, advisement, utilizing instructional resources, individualizing instruction, revising course syllabi, peer evaluation, and analyzing and giving feedback about student performance data.

   b. Became more positive about themselves and the program in general as a result of successful student performance on the NTE and faculty development sessions. They worked together to identify and agree upon higher performance goals for students to take the NTE and expected them to do well. Faculty members stopped complaining about what other colleges had not done properly to train and advise students, but rather began working with their colleagues across campus.

   c. Participated in the apportionment of competencies to various courses where they discovered redundancy in the teaching of some concepts and instructional gaps in others as implemented by them and their colleagues. They accepted responsibility for training toward newly assigned NTE generic skills competencies. Relatedly, they rewrote course syllabi to reflect both curriculum changes and the format of NTE test items. Faculty members also began to take advantage of the COE's Education Resource Center through frequent student referrals to these resources.

   d. Installed a new multiphased student advisement system. Faculty advisement responsibilities increased to include monitoring

112

recording grades, approving course schedules, and recommending students for student teaching and graduation. There was no accountability for advisement.

student progress beginning with the second semester of a student's freshman year. At various checkpoints in the system (entry to COE, the department, advanced standing, advanced methods, student teaching, and graduation), advisors are required to check and approve the student's advancement to the next step, building into the system needed accountability. Secondary education majors are coadvised by basic skills or arts and sciences and education faculty.

2. Students

a. Academic Standards. In 1980 students were admitted to teacher education with a minimum of 60 semester hours, a minimum GPA of 2.2 with no less than a grade of *C* in the English and professional sequences. They were required to have a 2.3 GPA for entry into student teaching and a 2.5 to graduate.

2. Students

a. Initiated new standards in 1980 which evolved over a six-year period to their present level as summarized here.
•A minimum 2.0 GPA for entry into the COE with passing scores on the COE basic skills tests.
•A minimum of 100 clock hours in early field-based experiences prior to student teaching.
•Successful passing of NTE's core battery by the end of the junior year and the complete examination prior to graduation.
•A minimum GPA of 2.5 for entry into teacher education, advanced standing, advanced methods, student teaching, and to graduate.
•Throughout their studies students are required to pass pre/post departmental subject matter and general knowledge tests and a comprehensive examination prior to graduation.

b. Academic Performance. Large numbers of students entered the college reading below the 12th grade level and few students were found to be writing at the college level. Mathematics percentile scores echoed reading and writing score data. The mean composite ACT score for GSU was 11 and for the COE 10. Grambling had an average six percent passing rate on the

b. Increased COE admission standards, remediation, increased course requirements, and other program improvements contributed to increasing students' reading, writing, and general academic performance above the 12th grade level. NTE performance increased to an average 100% pass rate and students now

113

NTE. Students seldom completed NTE in the time allotted. Except for 1978 between 1976 and 1980 students scored lower on the professional education portion of the NTE than they did in any other area. Entry level GPA's ranged from 1.5 to 4.0 with a large percentage at the lower end. Also in 1978 only 6 of 167 (or 3%) students who graduated passed the NTE and were eligible for certification and licensure.

c. Attitudes. Many student were un-motivated, had poor study habits, entered teaching as a last resort or because they lacked specific career goals. Additionally, they held few, if any, performance standards for them-selves and frequently failed to attend classes. They demonstrated little respect for instructors and instruction.

d. Acceptance of Professional Respon-sibility. Students were admitted to the COE at the beginning of their junior year and seldom explored or showed interest in the profession before then.

score lowest on the NTE in mathematics. Entry level GPA's have increased to an average of of 2.75. Students with less than a 2.5 are no longer admitted to the program.
•Because of improved reading skills, most students began com-pleting the entire test or scoring well enough to qualify for certification.
•Testing sophistication has improved.
•Students have increased the time they devote to studying and utilizing COE academic support services.
Note: All program graduates are required to pass all appropriate modules of the NTE as a condition for graduation.

c. Implemented higher performance standards for college and program admissions and course work effected more positive student attitudes. Student motivation for getting into teaching, respect for the program and instructors changed. They began to set higher performance standards for themselves and assumed a more professional attitude in both behavior and dress. Class attendance increased. Students began to depend less on them-selves and more on faculty for advisement and counseling. This led students to taking an im-proved sequence of courses.

d. Earlier acceptance of professional responsibility. Following pro-gram improvement efforts and evidence of peers passing the NTE, students were motivated to join COE student organizations and to inquire about COE admis-sions prior to the time for applying. Because the intro-ductory course to teaching was installed at the freshman level, students began to explore and show interest in teaching earlier

114

D. Resources

1. Data Base. Before 1980 the COE did not have an organized data base on student or faculty performance and failed to use the data that were available. Research activities were scattered and highly personal. Similarly, program evaluation data were almost nonexistent.

2. Dissemination of Information. Memorandums, faculty meetings, and limited scholarly presentations at local, regional, and national meetings by a few faculty members were the primary modes of disseminating information. Faculty development workshops in the COE were minimal. Information to students was largely communicated through advisory conference and bulletin boards. Dissemination audiences on campus mainly involved those in the COE.

3. Equipment. The COE owned one copier, one ditto machine, one small binder, one 16mm projector, two working overhead projectors, and no computers.

4. COE Student Faculty Support Services. The COE operated a small one-room curriculum resource center of mainly print materials and teacher aids.

in their academic careers. Students began studying for and taking the NTE earlier without prompting from faculty and administrators.

D. Resources

1. Developed and used a comprehensive data base. In 1980 a systematic research program focusing on students, faculty, curriculum, instruction, and advisement was implemented. This data base facilitated program improvement and helped to influence faculty ownership in the student performance problem.

2. Expanded the COE's dissemination of information via written reports, universitywide meetings and workshops, and hosting regional and national conferences. The content of this information included student performance data, NTE training materials, research based instructional techniques, and research on teacher education. Additionally, the college initiated and published each semester a COE newsletter for national audiences.

3. Acquired four copiers, 25 computers, video taping equipment, a heavy duty binder, and ten memorywriters through external funds and university support. Additionally, the amount of consumable supplies for COE faculty increased significantly.

4. Developed 5 classrooms into an Education Resource Center (ERC), with five laboratories (computer, tutorial, media, materials development, and teaching resource). The ERC also provided for diagnostic services, and the completion of student/faculty contracts. Simulated model classrooms (grades K-12) were developed and furnished for demonstrations and student practice.

5. External Consultants. The COE used short-term consultants for special meetings and conferences.	5. Hired short- and long-term consultants to provide a systematic program of faculty and organizational development for reforming the college. These consultants worked with faculty and students in small and large work groups.

These outcomes show that Grambling's strategy was effective for Grambling. They show further that Grambling was successful in achieving its major goal: to improve consistently the academic performance of students to a point of being able to claim excellence in teacher education.

Despite performance being the primary target of reform efforts, Grambling obviously looked beyond this variable in measuring effectiveness and success. The attitudes of faculty and students and changes in the capacity of the college organization to effect positive outcomes also were taken into consideration. In essence, the improvement strategy was evaluated for its comprehensive impact. The data attest to the comprehensiveness of both the strategy employed and the pervasiveness of its effects.

It is believed that Grambling's strategy was effective and successful for a variety of reasons, which include:

- The unique support and cooperation of central administration and other academic support units across campus

- The renaming of the entire teacher education program

- The maverick-like approach of the dean and a small leadership team

- The philosophical base on which the program was built and the ability to get faculty to buy into this philosophy

- The technical assistance provided by the long-term consultant, which constantly focused on developing and maintaining a healthy organization

- The college's success in acquiring resources

- Leadership that changed the college from a closed to an open system, ultimately, making it possible to induce new ideas and information

- A desire on the part of leadership and a critical mass of people to be "winners"–to have a quality teacher education program

LESSONS LEARNED

Do the ends always justify and subordinate the means? Is there something of value to be learned from the means? Faculty members and administrators at Grambling are interested in more than just the outcomes of their eight-year effort to achieve excellence in teacher education. Ends alone do not always justify the means. Insensitivity to the means leaves potentially successful outcomes too much to chance, subordinates human well-being to materialism, and increases the temptation to ignore, rather than to eliminate, obstacles to excellence.

To be successful, reformers must learn from their experiences. Scrutinizing the means of a reform effort provides more opportunities for acquiring such learnings than looking only at the ends. The College of Education questioned and studied both the processes and delivery systems continuously as it planned and implemented its innovations. For the first three of the past eight years, the college was engaged in program development and field testing what it thought would lead to excellence. Year four was devoted to refinement, and years five through eight focused on validation, institutionalization, and further fine-tuning. Years seven and eight focused on dissemination to other educational agencies and on refinement of program features.

Many lessons were learned as a result of these analyses. By dividing the college's work into yearly functions, an organizational schema for presenting the lessons derived from successes and failures naturally evolved. These lessons are presented below.

PROGRAM DEVELOPMENT

1. There had to be four levels of objectives: university, college, department, and individual. The objectives had to be related, made public, and monitored.

2. There had to be four levels of work carried on by each individual: for the university, for the college, for the department, and for self.

3. Everyone could not work on everything at the same time; effective goal-directed work transcended titles, job descriptions, and organizational charts. People had to be deployed to work in areas where they were needed and could make a contribution and where they demonstrated skill and expertise. The organization had to be kept functional and fluid at all times.

4. The university president, vice president for academic affairs and the whole central administrative team had to be involved in and committed to the college's educational reform movement early in the process to motivate the support of significant others.

5. Creative thinking and planning by the faculty were facilitated best by retreats (long or short) away form the every day work scene.

6. Tradition, personal goals, lack of professional integrity, established policies, lack of adequate funding, fear of the unknown and not knowing, and burnout were the most significant obstacles to the improvement process.

7. Mistakes could not be retrieved, so time could not be wasted on them; this time was better spent anticipating and preparing to deal with the consequences of mistakes.

8. Receptivity to new standards for student performance increased when students reflected the mutual identification and consensus of the faculty with consideration for university, state and national measures along with each faculty member's personal set of performance criteria.

9. People acted more quickly on the basis of concrete data that had direct implications for their past and future personal and professional behavior. Faculty members in the College of Education and across campus, as well as students, seemed more willing to change their behavior when they saw their performance outcomes in specific academic areas.

10. Frequent where-are-we meetings that focused on a previously written plan of action minimized procrastination, kept everyone informed, surfaced emergent problems, and facilitated the anticipation of future problems.

11. When faced with any change situation resembling an attack on personal integrity and academic ability, faculty members either withdrew or worked harder, but they always needed some form of sociopsychological guidance geared toward developing and maintaining positive self-concepts.

12. Admission, monitoring, retention, and exit criteria had been established, made public, revised as required, and reviewed over and over again.

13. Program innovations, i.e., remediation strategies, had to reflect consideration for the other academic commitments of students, not just in the College of Education. Heaping too many traditional responsibilities upon students tended to be self-defeating.

14. Optimum mileage from academic support systems was best achieved when they were guided by the College of Education in providing for the specific needs of the teaching majors.

15. Remediation activities had to involve more than faculty in the College of Education. They necessarily required the expertise of faculty in other colleges, whose involvement fostered further ownership in the problem and promoted a more cooperative working relationship among different campus units.

16. Students must be constantly apprised of the college's goals, successes, and changes. Special information sessions that bring all students together periodically during a semester greatly facilitate the exchange of such information.

17. Students and faculty need time to practice the new behaviors expected of them without penalties. Curriculum, instruction, and policy changes were followed much better when announced a minimum of one academic term prior to expectations for their formal implementation.

18. Clerical staff, graduate assistants, and students workers complete a number of tasks associated with program development. At appropriate points in the process, these persons have to be involved in information sessions that explain the college's goals, their goals and responsibilities, and acceptable standards for their performance.

19. When there are no incentives for developing quality programs, administrators must give some. For example:

Faculty Incentives

- Shared decision-making responsibilities
- Shared opportunities to serve as paid consultants
- Recognition in the college newsletter and on the campus radio station
- Summer employment through grants, etc.
- Allowing faculty to share ideas in open forums

Student Incentives

- Certificates of achievement
- Recognition in college newsletter, campus paper, and on campus radio

20. Incentives must also be given in the recruitment of academically talented students.

PROGRAM REFINEMENT

1. Program reviews, which encompassed component processes and achievements first, and the total program and related achievements second (a part-to-whole approach), tended to help people keep sight of the ultimate goal and the activities for achieving it.

2. At the point the program was to be refined, faculty and administrators tended to tire. Over- and under-doses of compliments on jobs well-done led to slippage, interim organizational inertia, and the temptation to rest on known successes—to relax while winning.

3. Historical records of change activities were invaluable resources for identifying areas for program refinement.

4. Mechanisms to maintain practices and processes the college wanted to institutionalize had to be developed and put into place early in the reform effort.

5. Just as maintenance mechanisms were developed to keep faculty members working toward goal achievement, similar mechanisms had to be put into place for students.

6. A primary means of realizing improvement was replacing ill working parts. Management had to replace people, processes, ideas and materials, but this action was made more palatable by giving reasons for these changes.

7. Pictures are indeed worth a thousand words. When steps in all new processes were flow-charted and faculty and students were taken through them several times, desired outcomes were more positive.

PROGRAM VALIDATION

1. Program validation provided answers to several key questions: (a) What did the college do? (b) How did the new program differ from the traditional program? (c) What were the planned

and unplanned outcomes of program improvement efforts? (d) What parts of the new program should the college institutionalize?

2. For validation to be effective, a variety of data collection methods was required: (a) a synthesis of college records and literature; (b) student and faculty interviews; (c) documentation of replicated analyses of the college's program with the programs of several other similar institutions; and (d) cross-validation of findings through planned internal and external evaluation activities.

3. It was validation together with ongoing evaluation that confirmed what was believed to have been accomplished and that supported images of credibility among observers internal and external to the university.

INSTITUTIONALIZATION

Institutionalization must be just as planned, deliberate, and organized as initial program development efforts, and it must involve the same academic units that contribute to program innovations. And, it requires the generation of as much ownership in the problem–institutionalization–as was generated in program development stages. In theory, institutionalization should begin at the outset of a change project. Experience taught that this is not possible in every situation. Rather, the readiness of the organization and the innovation for institutionalization are the deciding factors for when to institutionalize.

IMPLICATIONS

This analysis of program outcomes and lessons learned has many implications for other institutions interested in improving their teacher education programs. Clearly, such an improvement endeavor will be a complex, multifaceted process fraught with stumbling blocks that must be removed. It will require a long-term commitment that focuses on people and programs. People change and, in turn, people change programs with their new behaviors. Colleges of education cannot and should not try to do the job alone–the training of teachers is a universitywide responsibility. Nonetheless, colleges of education must provide the leadership to those who would cooperate and stimulate a spirit of cooperation in those who resist. This leadership should begin with a strong dean building a critical mass of change agents–people who are willing to violate traditional norms for the sake of progress; who are hard-working and desirous of winning; who can stay alive and fully functioning over time and not succumb to impediments and disappointments.

Central administration must be in the forefront of those who must be involved, and everyone must understand the relevant issues.

Unwritten norms, such as making change information public, practicing freedom to learn, and reaching out for assistance, support program improvement efforts. So do multiple communication channels and a well-developed accountability system for students and faculty.

Implied further is that a number of organizational development issues must be resolved if colleges of education are to be involved meaningfully in improving their teacher education program. This suggests a final note regarding the one discovery Grambling made over and over again: Adequate organizational health within the College of Education is the lifeblood of effective reform. Without it, things are bound to go awry. Highly skilled assistance is desirable in this area. When this expertise does not exist on campus, there should be no hesitancy in importing it. In fact, it is probably more desirable to secure this assistance from the outside.

Grambling went in search of excellence in teacher education. It took longer in coming than everyone would have liked, and it surprised all when it did come, but arrive it did. With it came the greatest lesson of all, excellence is achievable. The real challenge now is to minimize slippage and improve upon it.

CONSULTANT'S NOTE #5:

LOOKING TOWARD ORGANIZATIONAL INDEPENDENCE

My role at Grambling involves consultant-trainer functions. Not only am I charged with sharing my organization development knowledge, skills, ideas, and feelings, but also there are expectations that upon my exit, the system will be competent in most of these same areas. In essence, it is incumbent upon me to assist the COE organization and the system of teacher education in this organization renewal process so that the two will be capable of applying independently what they learned to new problems and opportunities.

After eight years, it is appropriate to question the success of my relationship with Grambling. Has the COE and the system of teacher education achieved the desired level of organizational independence that we have been working toward? Have appreciable changes been made in the system's structures, strategies, and processes? Has the system's level of effectiveness increased? What about the COE's organizational health, has it improved? And what does the system's future look like? This entry, the last of my notes, responds to these questions.

ORGANIZATIONAL FITNESS, EFFECTIVENESS, AND CHANGEABILITY

By now the success of Grambling's efforts to improve student performance on the NTE is fairly public. We can conclude from this indicator that the COE's organizational health improved enough to facilitate an effective system of teacher education. Perhaps not so common, however, is public knowledge of improvements in (1) the COE's capacity to maintain its effectiveness, (2) the COE's potential for helping the total teacher education system to maintain its effectiveness, and (3) the COE and the teacher education system's ability to adapt to new changes and demands from the environment.

Several indicators demonstrate that the COE and teacher education system are effective in these three areas. First is the leadership team, which has become a close knit group, highly skilled in assessing both its health and effectiveness. It is equally talented in planning for the organization and helping the system adapt to new demands and conditions. This team is not a finite group or a static membership. Depending upon the problem or issues, membership changes.

Second are the periodic major system audits the COE sponsors to look at itself. Usually, the audits are conducted by external evaluators representing a cross-section of the academic community: the public school sector, higher education, etc. An audit may focus upon the system of teacher education, the COE organization, a program, or an activity within a program. It may be requested by the dean, the leadership team or an academic unit. Audit results are made public, and identified problems are addressed in problem-solving sessions.

Third is increased participation in formal and informal research to constantly feed the creativity of the system. Central administration supports this activity by offering release time and competitive, mini-research grants to faculty members. This activity is above and beyond the college's continuous research activities centering on student performance.

Fourth is an ongoing, organized image improvement program based on effective communication inside and outside the university, an extensive networking system and high visibility in significant professional organizations and learned societies. The benefits of this approach are many: It feeds the organization's creativity, helps faculty and students maintain positive self-concepts, prevents the COE from returning to its near-closed system status, and keeps the organization energized with challenges to explore new ideas and relationships.

Fifth is the COE's "medicare" plan. By investing in the plan from time to time with newly acquired grants, the college is able to call upon outside expertise—consultants, when necessary, to retrain faculty or to assist in developing new major undertaking such as academic programs and service projects. Once this short-term input is received, the organization makes its action plan and creates its future.

Sixth are the new norms of internal connectedness and collective efficiency the COE practices. Programming, supplies and materials, as well as personnel are managed according to these two standards. By keeping the whole picture of COE and system-level activities in view, there is less chance of polarization and the waste of already limited resources.

There are variations in the COE's degree of growth in certain organizational development areas. The college made great strides, for example, in learning to maintain its health and effectiveness; but in my estimation, the organizational processes we went through were learned by only part of the organization's members. Those who know are applying them not only to NTE scores, but also to the quest for success with new programs. To the college's credit, nevertheless, those in the know help those who continue to learn, thereby decreasing the organization's dependency upon my services.

One area that continues to receive much attention from me, however, is human resource development, specifically as it pertains to helping the COE develop its leadership base. The COE's growth toward new programs and challenges and the attrition of existing personnel somewhat dictate this expansion.

One of the things that I have discussed with the dean and the existing leadership team is that new leaders must be socialized. By new leaders, I mean new to the position, not just new to the COE or the institution. Regardless of where the leaders come from, they must be taught the COE's organizational development processes, norms, philosophy, and principles of existence. New leaders also need to know the COE's existing programs as well as its plans and visions of the future. With this type of anchoring, the entry of new leaders will induce less stress on the organization. And the people themselves will be able to see more clearly how they fit into the plan. Thus, it is an investment in people with the potential for bringing great returns–an investment that cannot be taken lightly.

The problem of visibility of Grambling's success also demands that the dean and central administration continue to seek out and develop leaders. As the Grambling success story continues to spread, offers will come to some of its leaders, as well as to the dean himself. Maintaining present gains without existing leadership may be a very difficult task unless this expansion in leadership is achieved. Like anything else, expanding an organization's leadership calls for a plan. Proper socialization into leadership roles and gradual induction of new people into daily routines and tasks are primary responsibilities of existing leaders. While this idea seems promising, it is still under consideration; as usual, the COE has had to turn its energies to other things. Ironically, this delay demonstrates further the need that led to this exploration in the first place: For some organizations–like Grambling–there just never seems to be enough leaders to go around.

GRAMBLING'S FUTURE LOOKS BRIGHT

For obvious reasons, I am probably biased in looking at the future of Grambling's COE. Nonetheless, I admit to feeling that the college's future is bright. The system of teacher education is clear about what it intends to do and people understand what is expected of them. The college's curriculum offers more content, and even more significant, the students can learn more. Having a faculty that can see their contributions, better understand teacher education, and teach better has brought about these positive outcomes. Faculty members follow through now more than ever before on matters of teaching and learning and in matters that affect the health of their organization.

Given all this growth, nothing was sacrificed. Everyone came out a winner. It is a funny thing about winners, they enjoy winning; they seek out challenges; and the more they win, the harder they work to win. Thus, there is reason to believe that Grambling will continue to be a winner. It will continue to make significant contributions to the profession of teacher education.

And what will be my role in Grambling's future? From the outside looking in–who knows? It could be time to exit.

EPILOGUE

Excellence in teacher education is achieved not by luck, but by hard work; not by books, but by people; not by meeting a set of standards, but by setting and achieving standards that require far more than those already in existence; not by treating only activities, but by treating and revamping an entire program when necessary; not by hiding program deficiencies, but by seeking them out and dealing with them; and not by running from additional responsibility, but by adapting to and conquering challenges in a manner that supports and advances the profession. These things the College of Education at Grambling has learned in its eight-year struggle to improve its teacher education program.

The challenges that now confront the college focus on both old and new struggles for excellence. For instance, a number one priority is to maintain the College's effectiveness–to ensure that students and faculty members continue to perform adequately, not to rest with "well enough." For example, the College has recently piloted other program features designed to maintain effectiveness and elevate efficiency: 1. The Centralized Advisement, Referral, and Evaluation Center (CARE) was designed and installed to improve effectiveness in student admissions, monitoring, advisement, record-keeping, and other forms of support. 2. The College piloted additional requirements for observation-participation activities, computer literacy and instructional computing activities, and for taking specified components of the NTE at earlier points in the professional course sequence. Inherent in maintaining effectiveness is a need for constant renewing and upgrading of people's skills and of the organization's capacity for solving problems. The College is prepared to meet these challenges.

At the same time, though, the college is challenged to live out its broader mission: to provide quality teachers, not just for Louisiana, but for the nation and the world. In 1980, Grambling's College of Education was limited in its capacity to respond to this aspect of its mission. Today, the college is developing its resources and beginning to implement programs to work toward this mission. It is responding to the needs of the profession at both national and international levels.

Responding to the nation's shortage of trained personnel to serve underprepared postsecondary students, the college designed and installed three new graduate programs in developmental education. The master's and specialist degree programs were installed in fall 1983 and fall 1984, respectively. The doctor of education degree program, one-of-a-kind in the nation, was initiated in fall 1986.

Further work at the national level includes the development and dissemination of this document to our varied professional publics. Relatedly, the college is striving to develop projects that will allow it to provide technical assistance and dissemination services to other institutions improving their teacher preparation programs. These efforts go beyond those responses the college has made already to numerous requests for written information about its program and to requests for on-site visits from other institutions. There is an obvious need for this type of unselfish sharing, and Grambling is responding–in Texas, Alabama, Mississippi, Virginia, California, Tennessee, Arkansas, Missouri, Arizona–wherever and whenever it can.

New international initiatives, though not yet well focused, now include China, Africa, and Grenada. In addition to sharing our expertise and learning from these relationships, as we travel and work abroad, the college is welcoming international students to its campus.

The college is sensitive to all efforts to improve teacher education in general and to improve the training of minority teachers in particular. Hence, this explanation of what Grambling did to make a difference. Our hope is that this document will make a difference over and over again in the professional lives of those who use it to guide their future efforts.

REFERENCES

Allen, D. and Seifman, E. The Teacher's Handbook. Glenview, Illinois: Scott, Foresman and Company, 1971.

Allport, Gordon W. The Nature of Prejudice. Garden City, New York: Doubleday Anchor, 1958.

Beckhard, R. Organization Development: Strategies and Models. Reading, Massachusetts: Addison-Wesley, 1969.

Ebel, R. L. The Uses of Standardized Testing. Bloomington, Indiana: Phi Delta Kappan Education Foundation, 1977.

French, L. & Bell, H. Organization Development: Behavioral Science Interventions for Organizational Improvement. Englewood Cliffs, New Jersey: Prentice Hall, 1978.

Gross, N., Giacquinta, J. B., and Berstein, M. Failure to implement a major organizational innovation. In J. V. Baldridge and T. E. Deal (Eds.), Managing Change in Educational Organization. Berkeley, California: McCutchan.

Gubser, L. Competency testing and national accreditation in teacher education. Action in Teacher Education, 1979 (Spring-Summer), 1, 21-27.

Hunter, M. Motivation Theory for Teachers. El Segundo, California: TIP Publications, 1979.

Huse, E. F. Organization Development and Change. New York: West Publishing Company, 1980.

Klemp, G. O. Three factors of success in the world of work: Implications for curriculum in higher education. Presentation made at the Annual Convention of the American Association of Higher Education, Chicago, Illinois, March 1977.

Lewin, K. Field Theory in the Social Sciences. New York: Harper & Row, 1951.

Lyons, G. Why teachers can't teach. Texas Monthly, September 1979, 122-128 and 208-220.

Pipho, C. Testing the teaching profession. <u>Phi Delta Kappan</u>, 1979, <u>66</u>, 597-598.

Pottinger, P. S. Competency assessment at school and work. <u>Social Policy</u>, September/October 1977, <u>8</u> (2), 35-40

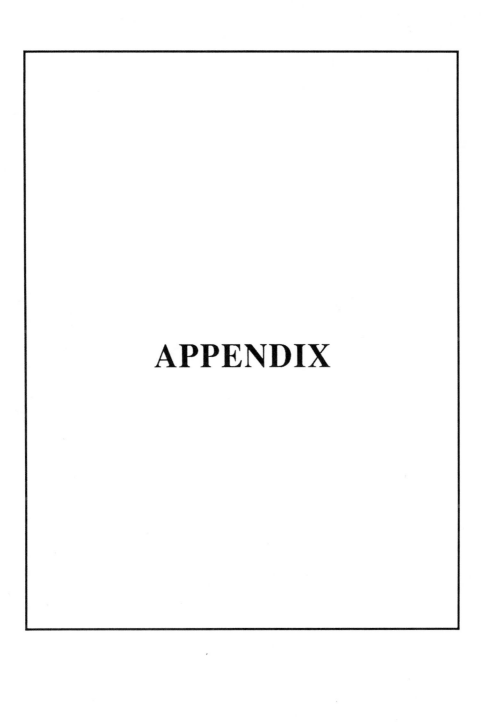

APPENDIX

A LETTER TO TEACHER EDUCATORS

Dear Teacher Educators:

Ours is an old and honored profession that has withstood the uncertain times, the good times, and the turbulent times. We have gone full cycle. Now we are again in the midst of turbulent times characterized by erosion of our profession's quality and ranks.

Interestingly, we no longer appear to be working diligently for curriculum innovations, race desegregation, student retention, discipline strategies, sex desegregation, or even refinement of a pedagogy of teaching. These problems, though virtually unsolved, have had to be tucked away for a later cycle. Perhaps this was to be expected. The winds of change have shifted. In their stead have loomed problems much larger and much more exigent than ever before: an increasing teacher shortage, devastating attacks on the competency of teachers and teacher educators, dismantling of teacher training institutions, a syphoning off of teacher talent by other professions, demands to turn over the training of teachers to public schools, alternative certification schemes that tend to devalue traditional teacher education majors in favor of arts and science majors, and teacher tests that are fast bringing Black teachers and historically Black institutions to the brink of extinction. Obviously, these are problems of a different sort, the kind that threatens the very life line of education.

In the past, the profession has survived many adversaties. Often this survival resulted from dialogue or innovative action that brought us redemption time. We had time to renew our defenses. We had time to experiment with cures for the profession's organizational ills, and we have time to apply Band-aids to curriculum and instructional blemishes. Peculiarly harsh public responses to our contemporary problems, however, suggest that there is not time for negotiating. There is time only for documenting evidence that colleges of education (COEs) can, in fact, produce competent teachers.

More to the point, society has demonstrated over and over the need for quality teachers reflecting all the diverse segments of the American population. We have been slow as a profession to comprehend fully that this diversity necessarily includes Black teachers. As a profession, we cannot afford to lose our Black teachers or our historically Black teacher training institutions. But lose them we will if we continue doing nothing. The destructive fallout of such a loss is inescapable by any of us in the profession, Black or White. Odds are that a ripple effect will cause everyone to suffer irreparable losses. A look at the impact of societal forces on Blacks, for example, demonstrates how grave the situation is.

While the number of minority children in school is increasing, the number of minority preservice teachers is steadily declining. The National Center for Education Statistics indicated that only 12 percent of the national teaching force is minority; the number of Black minority teachers is estimated at 8.6 percent. Further, in 1970, Black children comprised 14.9 percent of the total public school enrollment. By 1990, the center predicted that Blacks will constitute more than 30 percent of the school-aged population, while less than 5 percent of the nation's teachers will be Black.

For Black teacher training colleges, the statistics are as dismal. In 1959, 52 percent of the graduates at Black institutions were in education; in 1979, the comparable figure was 26 percent. Of the 11,510 Black education majors in 1979, Black institutions trained nearly 50 percent. With the advent of teacher tests, Black teachers started disappearing and Black college enrollments started declining. The number of education majors at Texas Southern dropped from 800 out of 4,000 ten years ago to 400 out of 8,000 in 1982 (Education Week, March 1982); and at Florida A&M from 1,000 in 1979 to 400 in 1982 (Tallahassee Democrat, January, 1982). These are but two examples of similar predicaments across the nation. Probable consequences? Closure or decertification of Black teacher training institutions. Since historically Black institutions contribute the greater percentage of minority teachers, the consequences of allowing them to be closed would be multifaceted and yield a lasting negative educational and cultural impact.

Why the decline in our Black teaching force? As mentioned, aside from gravitation to other professions, some Blacks are indeed the casualties of tests, either admission tests for entering teacher training programs or competency tests for exiting training programs and entering the profession. Statistics from various sources substantiate the inability of many Blacks successfully to negotiate competency tests for initial certification: (1) Georgia – 87 percent of the Whites, but only 34 percent of the Blacks passed a 1981 teacher competency tests on the first try; (2) California–71 percent of the Blacks, Hispanics, and non-Asian minorities failed a 1982 teacher competency test; (3) Florida – 37 percent of Florida A&M's and 18 percent of Bethune Cookman's candidates passed the state's 1981 teacher competency tests, while 88 percent of the Whites passed; and (4) Arkansas–51 percent of the Blacks taking a pilot NTE in 1983 scored poorly with 47 percent of this number noncertifiable.

Colleges of education are subcultures of the profession and may be distinguished by the dominant clientele their institutions serve. These distinctions traverse a continuum from ivy league schools, dominated by wealthy and academically talented students, to state-supported schools, dominated by the economically disadvantaged, ethnic minority, and academically marginal students taking advantage of open admission opportunities. It should not surprise anyone that the colleges of education suffering the biggest threat to survival are either predominantly and historically Black or those with open admissions; students from these institutions overwhelmingly cluster at the lower end of the economic ladder. Also, it should not be surprising that these colleges have larger numbers of less academically talented students than do ivy league and selected admission institutions.

Although there may be merit in competency tests, it is a fallacy to assume, as many people seem to have done, that an individual's test score represents the quality and consequently the value of the college from which the individual graduates. It is common knowledge that colleges of education share the training of teachers with other disciplines in other colleges. So why single out colleges of education to suffer alone such harsh punishment? For some, Tertullian (Third Century A.D.) offers an answer to this question:

> They take the Christians to be the cause of every disaster to the state, of every misfortune to the people. If the Tiber reaches the wall, if the Nile does not reach the fields, if the sky does not move or if the earth does, if there is famine, or if there is a plague, the cry is at once, "The Christians to the lions."

Others probably believe as did Shine and Goldman (1980). Commenting on competency testing in New Jersey public schools, they said much that has relevance for higher education:

> We believe it is a hoax to misuse psychometrics for political purposes, equating statistical gain on a single test with significant curriculum improvement. It is cruel because it demeans the arduous process of teaching and learning and gives the community the impression that public ridicule of educators can eliminate decades of societal neglect. (201)

The answer may be within the education profession itself. It is conceivable that colleges of education have been left alone to throw off the credulous consequences of test abuse because the profession has not yet considered this ramification. Closure of a COE for any reason, but especially as an immolative gesture toward accountability, is a serious indictment against all constituencies of the profession: the victimized colleges certainly, but also other colleges of education, the institutions to which these colleges belong, state education systems–the profession as a whole. If this perception is accurate, there is but one logical, yet alarming conclusion. The fall of a single college signals the beginning of the profession's fall. This blindness is a dispositional barrier for the profession that bespeaks a multifaceted problem in critical consciousness.

In 1979, Lyons shocked almost everyone when he claimed in his inflammatory presentation, "Why Teachers Can't Teach," that teacher colleges graduated "certified ignoramuses." Lyons was reacting in part to 50 percent of 535 first-year teachers failing a competency test administered by the Dallas Independent School District and to similar testing outcomes in Houston. He asserted further that such testing programs were created because school districts no longer trusted teacher colleges.

Whether to have or not to have competency testing for teacher candidates is not being debated on this occasion. Rather, the issue is **who** should be held accountable for the performance of teacher candidates on competency tests. As Lyons pointed out much too late in his article, the test used in Dallas (the Wesman Personnel Classification Test) "was not designed specifically to examine teacher competence." Like many of the tests–or components thereof–given teachers, the Wesman instrument measures general knowledge and fundamental skills in reasoning and mathematics. For most institutions, the primary responsibility for training in these areas rests with units other than colleges of education. Equally as important are these points:

- Most teacher education majors are required by state certification standards to receive more than half of their training (all of their training in the basic skills or general knowledge areas) outside colleges of education.

- The teacher education curriculum is actually governed by almost everyone but teacher education faculties.

- Colleges of education have little authority over the quality of training provided by departments outside of their own units.

- Colleges of education typically receive students during the last two years of their training careers, after they have received *A's*, *B's*, and *C's* in English, math, science, and social science.

If teacher training, curriculum development, and program governance are shared with other academic units, should not these units also share the responsibility of accountability? More fundamentally, why are those in the know about the academic functions of various units in higher education and the decentralized governance of teacher education so willing to stand back in silence and let colleges of education suffer or, even worse, participate in blaming and pointing fingers at them? Perhaps Allport's comments (1958) on scapegoating is an appropriate answer here. He stated:

> From earliest times the notion has persisted that guilt and misfortune can be shifted from one man's back to another. Animistic thinking confuses what is mental and with what is physical. If a load of wood can be shifted, why not a load of sorrow or a load of guilt?

There are those who would say that the problem of teacher shortages and Black teacher extinction can be solved simply by forgetting about tests. Yet, tests are as American these days as designer jeans, Coca Cola, and apple pie. We in education have used them in one form or another for decades. And in many ways, tests have helped to advance the profession toward its ultimate goal: producing quality teachers. Throwing teacher competency tests out the window does not seem a realistic solution to the problem. Rather, among other things, learning how to use tests to our advantage and using them more appropriately seem to offer a more permanent solution. This letter is a plea for the latter position.

Right now, we know that tests screen out both incompetent and competent teachers. We know that most tests are culturally biased. We know that paper and pencil tests cannot accurately measure teacher performance in the classroom. We know, whether we admit it or not, that when we begin to rely on test makers for our tests, we are, in fact, allowing them to dictate curricula to match their tests--to dictate what we teach in the classroom. We know that, unlike Coca Cola and apple pie, the mere mention of a test excites immobilizing fear in many people. For preservice teachers it is fear that a test score can label them failures and arbitrarily deny them access to a "professional life." In fact, it seems that the mental anguish caused by tests (before and after they are taken) can be so psychologically damaging that the Surgeon General would do well to stamp all tests, "Warning! Testing may be dangerous to your health and livelihood." Yes, we know the problems with tests, but few of us attempt to do anything about correcting these problems.

The belief is that the profession must not only work toward mastering testing technologies and bringing testing under control to save our teachers (particularly our Black teachers), but also it must implement more comprehensive teacher training improvement programs. To do this we must first internalize these facts: (1) testing is here to stay; (2) the fear of tests can be more damaging than the tests themselves; (3) tests for initial teacher certification represent not only the work of colleges of education, but also the work of those in public schools and in postsecondary institutions who provide for the general education of students as well; (4) tests often do point up (although we frequently deny it) weaknesses that need to be remedied in our teacher training curricula, thereby suggesting holistic curriculum reform instead of add-ons and short-term coaching; and (5) because colleges of education receive the most negative impact from testing fall out, it is these bodies that must take the reins of leadership to bring about reform in testing.

To be sure, these are turbulent times for teacher education. For the profession, especially its colleges of education, to be free of the threats posed by test abuse, the consciousness of the profession must be raised on several issues: shared accountability, collective efficiency, and revolutionary leadership. Grambling contributes this story as an exemplar of such raised consciousness. Other such stories are needed.

Johnnie Ruth Mills

ABOUT THE AUTHORS

Johnnie Ruth Mills, lead author for this book, has served as associate professor of education at Grambling State University; director of the Teacher Education Improvement Validation Project, and director of Graduate Programs in Developmental Education. She has special expertise in program development and evaluation in teacher education, multicultural education, and developmental education. While at Grambling, she made numerous national presentations on teacher education, trained educators at all levels of the profession, and served as a consultant for other higher education institutions in the areas of supervision, competency testing for teachers, and multicultural education. Her major publications include several articles in the <u>Journal of Teacher Education</u> and the <u>Journal of Social and Behavioral Science</u>. She has written a research monograph for the National Association for Developmental Education and several other literary works, including chapters for monographs sponsored by various other agencies. She holds the doctor of philosophy degree from Florida State University.

Dr. Mills is currently dean of the School of Education at Jackson State University of Mississippi.

Jo Ann Dauzat is a professor of education and director of Professional Laboratory Experiences at Grambling State University. She directed several teacher education improvement initiatives focusing on curriculum revision, instructional improvement, and student accountability, and she also has served as head of the Department of Teacher Education. She has written and co-written texts in reading and three work-text series for adult learners, as well as, articles in major journals such as the <u>Journal of Reading</u>. Her doctor of education degree is from Northeast Louisiana University.

Burnett Joiner is the executive dean of education at Grambling State University. It was under his leadership that the College of Education implemented its Teacher Education Improvement Project. At various points in his career, prior to working at Grambling, he served as teacher, principal, and assistant superintendent in several public school systems. He also served as a regional executive secretary for National Teacher Corps for three years. Additional experiences include consulting, training, and writing on various topics in teacher education at local, state, and national levels. He holds the doctor of philosophy degree from the University of South Carolina.

ABOUT THE CONTRIBUTORS

Jack Gant, who contributed the Consultant Notes for this book, is an organization development and management consultant. He served as dean of the College of Education at Florida State University and is a past president of the American Association of Colleges for Teacher Education (AACTE). Since leaving the deanship, he has built a rich background of consultation and training experiences in higher education, in both the United States and foreign countries. As core consultant for Grambling's teacher education improvement efforts, he provided long-term services to management and faculty. This relationship is ongoing. In the course of his career, he has published widely in the areas of organization development and teacher education.

Earline Simms served as professor of education at Grambling State University and head of the Department of Teacher Education. Her past experiences include consulting and writing for local, state, regional, and national audiences in these areas. She holds a doctor of philosophy degree from Kansas State University.

Dr. Simms is currently dean of Education at South Carolina State College.

ABOUT THE TECHNICAL EDITORS

Sharon Givens has served as the editor, photographer and coordinator of publications for the American Association of Colleges of Teacher Education for nine years. For three of those nine years, she was editor for the ERIC Clearinghouse on Teacher Education. She began her career as a newspaper reporter and editor in Kansas, and she holds the bachelor of journalism degree and the master of mass communication degree from the University of South Carolina.

Scott Dewbre is the editor for the Grambling State University College of Education, where he is responsible for the coordination of publications, media relations and promotions. Prior to working at Grambling, he wrote on education-related issues for eight years as a newspaper reporter and editor in Oklahoma, and he continued to work in education afterwards by moving into college public relations. He holds the bachelor of journalism degree from the University of Oklahoma.

CHECKLIST
COE ADMISSION AND MONITORING
(Teaching Majors)

Name _____   S.S. # _____

This student has:

By the end of freshman year

Yes No

_____ _____	Completed the Basic Studies requirements and applied for transfer
_____ _____	Completed COE Application for Admission
_____ _____	A minimum 2.0 GPA
_____ _____	Been admitted to COE: Conditional _____ Unconditional _____ Date _____
_____ _____	Passed the Reading Test (minimuim composite of 11.0) Date _____
	Passed the COE English Proficiency Test:
_____ _____	Essay Date_____
_____ _____	Objective Date_____
_____ _____	Passed the Math Proficiency Test Date_____
_____ _____	Taken Ed. 162–Introduction to Teaching
_____ _____	A COE advisor
_____ _____	Taken Communication Module of NTE Date_____
_____ _____	Completed 15 hrs. O/P

By end of sophomore year

Yes No

_____ _____	A minimum of 25 hours in Observation/Participation (Ed. 162 - 10 hrs.; Ed. 202 or 204 - 10 hrs.
	Passed NTE Modules: Date _____
_____ _____	Communication Skills (645) Date_____
_____ _____	General Knowledge (644) Date_____
_____ _____	Applied for admission to a teaching program Date_____
_____ _____	Had an admission interview
	Taken departmental tests:
_____ _____	Subject matter Pre _____ Post _____ Date_____
_____ _____	General Knowledge Pre _____ Post _____ Date_____
_____ _____	Professional Knowledge Pre _____ Post _____ Date_____
_____ _____	A minimum 2.5 GPA
_____ _____	Been admitted to a department (Degree Program) Date__

By end of junior year

Yes No

_____ _____	A minimum of "C" in complete English sequence
_____ _____	A minimum of "C" in any professional course
_____ _____	A minimum of "C" in any specialized academic course
_____ _____	Removed all academic deficiencies
	Taken departmental tests:
_____ _____	Subject matter Pre _____ Post _____ Date_____
_____ _____	General Knowledge Pre _____ Post _____ Date_____
_____ _____	Professional Knowledge Pre _____ Post _____ Date_____
_____ _____	A minimum of 30 Observation/Participation hours (Ed. 162, Ed. 200,Ed. 202 or 204, Ed. 300)
_____ _____	A major and minor (or concentration)
_____ _____	Applied for Admission to Advanced Standing Date _____
_____ _____	Been admitted to Advanced Standing Date _____
_____ _____	Completed Ed. 303, 314, 328, and 320, 322 or 325
_____ _____	Applied for and admitted to Advanced Methods Date _____

_____ _____ A minimum of 40 Observation/Participation hours (Ed. 314 and Ed. 402)

By end of first semester of senior year
Yes No

_____ _____ A minimum 2.5 GPA
_____ _____ Completed Advanced Methods course(s) with a minimum grade of "C"
_____ _____ Proficiency in communicative skills
_____ _____ Exhibited sound professional judgment
_____ _____ A minimum of 100 Observation/Participation hours
_____ _____ Take the departmental pretest   Date _____
_____ _____ Passed the Professional Knowledge Module of the NTE   Date _____
_____ _____ Completed specialized academic sequence with a minimum grade of "C"
_____ _____ Applied for Student Teaching   Date _____

By end of senior year
Yes No

_____ _____ A minimum 2.5 GPA
_____ _____ Completed an approved program
_____ _____ Passed the COE Senior Comprehensive
_____ _____ Taken the departmental Posttest   Date _____
_____ _____ Passed the Specialty Area of the NTE   Date _____
_____ _____ Applied for graduation   Date _____
_____ _____ Applied for certification   Date _____

My signature affirms that the information checked above is correct to the best of my knowledge.

_____
Student Signature

_____
Advisor

_____
Department Head

COE/FALL, 1985

APPLICATION FOR ADVANCED PROFESSIONAL
LABORATORY EXPERIENCES

COLLEGE OF EDUCATION
GRAMBLING STATE UNIVERSITY

Date of Application _____
Seeking Admission for F Sp S 19_____

(Please type or print neatly)

Name_____
      Last   First   Middle/Maiden
I.D. No_____SSN-_____
Home Address_____
 City_____State____Zip_____
Local Address_____
City_____State____Zip_____
Telephone No.: Home (____)_____
Local (____)_____
Marital Status_____
Do you have access to a car?_____
If you answer yes to any of the questions below,
explain on the back of this form.
Yes No
☐ ☐ 1. Do you have courses to take after this
      laboratory experience?
☐ ☐ 2. Do you plan to take a course with the labo-
      ratory experience?
☐ ☐ 3. Should your physical condition be consid-
      ered in your placement for the laboratory
      experience?

Area Adviser _____
COE Adviser _____
Major Field_____
Minor Field_____
Date Advanced Methods Taken _____Grade_____
GPA
NTE Core Battery Test Scores

_____   _____
General Knowledge   Communications

_____   _____
Professional Knowledge   O/P Hours Completed
Applying for admission to (Check appropriate areas)
☐ Student Teaching   ☐ Practicum
  ☐ Elementary   ☐ Special Ed.
  ☐ Early Childhood Ed. ☐ Early Childhood Ed.
  ☐ Special Ed.   ☐ Teacher Ed.
  ☐ Secondary Ed.   ☐ Library Ed.
☐ Internship
  ☐ Therapeutic Rec.
  ☐ Parks and Rec. Adm.
  ☐ Camping and Outdoor
  ☐ Other_____
Preferred Placement in order of priority
Parish _____ City _____
Parish _____ City _____
Parish _____ City _____
Preferred Grade Level (Circle one):
  K 1 2 3 4 5 6 7 8 9 10 11 12

To be completed by Area Adviser
☐ Admit ☐ Pending ☐ Do Not Admit
Comment:_____

_____

Signature _____
Date _____

To be completed by COE Adviser
☐ Admit ☐ Pending ☐ Do Not Admit
Comment: _____

_____

Signature_____
Date _____

To be completed by COE Department Head
☐ Admit ☐ Pending ☐ Do Not Admit
Comment:_____

_____

Signature_____
Date_____

To be completed by Director of OPLE
☐ Admit ☐ Pending ☐ Do Not Admit
Comment:_____

_____

Signature_____
Date _____

COLLEGE OF EDUCATION
GRAMBLING STATE UNIVERSITY

CURRICULUM CONTRACT

Department	Major	Minor	Classification	Semester
Year				

<u>**COURSES**</u>

1. _____

2. _____

3. _____

4. _____

5. _____

6. _____

7. _____

8. _____

9. _____

10. _____

COMMENTS: _____

_____

_____

_____

_____

_____

_____

Student: _____ I.D. No. _____ Date: _____

Advisor: _____ Date: _____

STUDENT/White ADVISOR/Green DEPARTMENT HEAD/Canary STUDENT SERVICES OFFICES/Pink ACADEMIC DEAN/Goldenrod

Application for Admittance to Advanced Teaching Methods Seminars: Elementary, Early Childhood, High School Subjects, and Special Education

Date of Application _____

Name _____ I.D. No. _____
      Last   First   Middle

Name of COE Adviser _____

Name of Major Area Adviser _____

Major Field _____

Semester Enrollment is Requested _____

Age _____ Marital Status _____

Permanent Address _____
          (P.O. Box/Street)   (City/State)   (Phone)

Local Address _____
         (P.O. Box/Street)   (City/State)   (Phone)

Do you have access to a car? _____

COE Department in which you are enrolled _____

Date Admitted to Teacher Education _____ Scholastic Average _____

Date Admitted to Advanced Standing _____

Health? Excellent _____ Good _____ Fair _____ Physical Defects _____
                                               Describe in next section)

Comments by applicant for special consideration:

Approval Schedule	Do not Admit	Admit	Signature	Date
1. Receipt of OPLE	_____	_____	_____	_____
2. Area	_____	_____	_____	_____
3. COE Adviser	_____	_____	_____	_____
4. COE Department Head	_____	_____	_____	_____
5. OPLE Director	_____	_____	_____	_____
6. Notification by mail (Student,	_____	_____	_____	_____

COMMENTS: Please make comments on the appraisal form.

AUTOBIOGRAPHICAL INFORMATION

DATE _____

Your Name _____   Date of Birth _____

Name of parents or Guardians: _____

Marital Status (check one) [ ]   Married   [ ] Single   [ ] Divorced

Name of Spouse: _____

Names of Children (if any): _____

Hobbies: _____

Special Non-Teaching Skills: _____

Previous Work Experiences: _____

_____

Are there other teachers in your family? _____   How many? _____

Education (State briefly high points of each level):

    A. Elementary (give name of school and dates of attendance):

    B. Secondary (give name of school and dates of attendance):

    C. College (give name of college and dates of attendance):

Desired Level of Certification

    A. Elementary (give level): _____   Minor: _____

    B. Secondary (give fields):   Major: _____

                              Minor: _____

What are your career plans after graduation?

_____

_____

APPRAISAL FORM FOR ADMISSION TO STUDENT TEACHING

Name of Student _____

                              Last   First   Middle

_____   _____

               Major   Minor or Concentration (Circle One)

Academic Average   _____   Methods Grade   _____

I. Fill in each blank with "YES" or "NO" for the following items:

    _____   1. Has been admitted to Advanced Standing

    _____   2. Has completed appropriate Methods Course(s) with a minimum grade of "C"

    _____   3. Has completed appropriate specialized academic courses with a minimum grade fo "C"

    _____   4. Has a minimum grade-point average of 2.5

    _____   5. Has no handicapping conditions which would interfere with effective teaching

    _____   6. Has general proficiency in communicative skills

    _____   7. Has demonstrated social and emotional maturity

    _____   8. Has completed the observation-participation requirement (Minimum of 100 clock hours)

    _____   9. Has on file pre and post departmental test scores for the junior year

    _____ 10. Has taken the Professional Knowledge Module of the NTE

    _____ 11. Has demonstrated exemplary moral and ethical character

II. **Courses to be taken:**

    1. Courses to be taken <u>along with</u> Student Teaching (based upon a review of the student's transcript):

        _____

        _____

        _____

    2. Courses to be taken <u>after</u> Student Teaching (based upon a review of the student's transcript):

        _____

        _____

        _____

III. **Recommendation:** (Check one)

    _____   This students meets the eligibility criteria for admission to Student Teaching. I recommend that he/she be admitted.

    _____   This student does <u>not</u> meet the eligibility criteria for admission to student teaching. I do <u>not</u> recommend admission.

                                 _____

                                 Advisor

                                 _____

                                 Department Head

NOTE: A copy of this form should also be completed by the liaison faculty advisor and department head for secondary education majors.

APPRAISAL FORM FOR ADMISSION TO METHODS COURSES

Name of Student _____   Date _____

Major _____   Minor _____

I. **Fill each blank below with "YES" or "NO" for the following items:**

_____ 1. Has been admitted to Teacher Education

_____ 2. Has been admitted to Advanced Standing

_____ 3. Has a minimum grade of "C" in each professional course

_____ 4. Has a minimum grade of "C" in specialized academic courses

_____ 5. Has a minimum grade of "C" in English sequence

_____ 6. Has a minimum GPA of 2.3

_____ 7. Is free from handicapping conditions that would interfere with effective teaching

_____ 8. Has passed the English Proficiency Test

_____ 9. Has passed the Mathematics Proficiency Test

_____ 10. Has an acceptable reading score

_____ 11. Has passed the NTE Communication Skills Test

_____ 12. Has passed the NTE General Knowledge Test

_____ 13. Has on file Pre- and Postdepartmental test scores for the sophomore year

_____ 14. Has a major and minor (or concentration) area of study

_____ 15. Has completed a minimum of 40 hours of observation and participation experiences

_____ 16. Has completed Edu. 303, 314, 320, 322, and 325

II. **Comments: Strengths and/or weaknesses of the student:**

III. **Recommendation: (Check One)**

_____ This students meets the eligibility criteria for admission to advanced methods. I recommend that he/she be admitted.

_____ This student does not meet the eligibility criteria for admission to advanced methods. I do not recommend admission.

_____
Advisor

_____
Department Head

NOTE: A copy of this form should be completed by the liaison faculty advisor and department head for secondary education majors.